MENTORING

Helping Employees Reach Their Full Potential

Gordon F. Shea

AMA Management Briefing

AMA MEMBERSHIP PUBLICATIONS DIVISION
AMERICAN MANAGEMENT ASSOCIATION

For information on how to order additional copies of this publication, see page 93.

Library of Congress Cataloging-in-Publication Data

Shea, Gordon F. , 1925-
  Mentoring : helping employees reach their full potential
Gordon F. Shea
    p. cm. —(AMA management briefing)
    ISBN 0-8144-2357-4 : $14.95
    1. Mentors in business. 2. Employees —Training of. 3. Employees-
  Counseling of. I. Title. II. Series.
HF5385.S55 1994
658.4' 07124—dc20   94-36222
                                                          CIP

First printing.

FTW
AFJ 8093

Contents

Introduction

Since the mid-1980s, the employee-development strategy known as *mentoring* has changed dramatically. Mentoring has progressed from a Machine-Age model to an Information-Age model, and this new form of helping people learn offers a wealth of management opportunities for organizational rejuvenation, competitive adaptation, and employee development.

Much of this change has occurred in response to significant developments affecting organizations overall, including operational and technological advancements, evolutions in local and world markets, and an entire set of new workplace realities— downsizings, delayerings, restructurings, reengineering, and the like.

The problem is, many organizations appear to have missed a curve in the road. They are unaware of the new model and the promise it holds.

To appreciate how mentoring has changed, and to understand how organizations have responded to that change, consider the results of two research studies, one conducted in 1984 and the other in early 1994.

The first (1984) study polled human resources directors at 62 firms and 37 government agencies (Federal, state, and local) in the greater Washington, D.C./Baltimore area about their use of mentoring as an employee-development tool. The researcher drew his sample from a variety of private sector organizations (company sizes ranged from approximately 100 employees to more than 2,000), and he selected public sector agencies so that the response group would represent significant segments of government. For example, at the Federal level, respondents came from agencies within the U.S. Department of Transportation and U.S. Department of Agriculture; at the state and local levels, it was the Highway and Police Departments. (The researcher chose to use such organizational units because they were small enough so that someone near the top could answer specific questions.)

Overall, the researcher found that the HR directors had little specific knowledge about mentoring activities within their organizations. Many made vague references to their efforts in "encouraging informal mentoring." Six respondents (about 10 percent) said their firms did have mentoring programs in place. In all cases, these respondents worked in large, stable, "old line" organizations that used mentoring to:

• *Initiate and Orient New Professional Hires.* The organizations matched these employees, usually referred to as interns, with higher level people outside of their "chain of command" for a period of three months to a year.

• *Develop High-Potential Personnel.* The organizations singled out certain individuals to be "fast tracked" for management positions and often assigned them a mentor to help them in their climb up the career ladder.

• *Assist in Succession Planning.* Three organizations had an informal custom whereby management and executive personnel trained their successors. The mentors in these relationships were not actually trained to mentor; instead, they generally engaged in a "Copy what I do and how I do it" type of activity.

The government sampling, in contrast, failed to reveal

any meaningful patterns, with one exception: Many police departments promoted the mentoring of new personnel (especially personnel who were new to patrol) by experienced officers. Respondents from many of the other agencies seemed uncertain as to whether the organization did or did not use mentoring.

The 1994 study, which attempted to access the same organizations (six of the companies had disappeared, moved, or been absorbed by others, and two government units had merged with another organization), produced substantial contrasts.

Specifically, of the 56 private firms that responded for a second time, one-third reported they now had formal mentoring programs in place, and another third were actively exploring such programs. Of the 35 government agencies that responded for a second time, 17 said they now had some form of mentoring in place, and 15 said they were exploring the possibilities.

Although the survey worked with a limited sample, the results mirror the growth, nationwide, in mentoring during this time frame. What is more interesting—and a bit disturbing—is that, of all the organizations that had adopted some form of mentoring, half of the programs clearly resembled the Machine-Age model. Moreover, almost all the other organizations seemed to be struggling to adapt the old model to new needs. Very few demonstrated awareness that a more forward-looking model was available. The two approaches stand in sharp contrast, as the following discussion shows.

CHARACTERISTICS OF THE MACHINE-AGE MODEL

The Machine-Age model of mentoring is closely associated with general descriptions of the Industrial Age. For example, the model is characterized by:

• *A single-minded focus on career advancement.* The model assumes that employees are seeking to climb an organizational ladder within the tall, hierarchical, multi-layered, organization of the past.

• *The perception that a mentor is a protector and sponsor.* The model refers to the mentor's charge by the medieval term "protege" (literally, "the protected one"). Historically, the protege's career was placed in the hands of a more powerful advocate (who, ironically, had sometimes used the protege as a pawn in empire building and office politics).

• *A tendency to clone look-alike, think-alike, and act-alike managers.* The model encourages managers to share a particular organizational vision and culture, and to hold similar career aspirations.

• *A vision of mentoring that is fundamentally elitist.* According to this model, mentoring is a strategy for assimilating "high potential" personnel, rather than a tool for discovering or developing varied talents throughout the workforce.

• *The exclusion of broader, organizational concerns.* Because of its emphasis on an individual's career-development goals, the Machine-Age model overlooked the importance of mentoring to organization development. This may explain why many upper level managers resisted formal mentoring programs during the Industrial Age.

• *A preoccupation with the rationalization of work, logical problem solving, and the "dumbing down" of jobs.* During the Industrial Age, this preoccupation left little besides a paycheck for the millions of employees who either applied their imagination, enthusiasm, ideas, and talents to ventures outside the workplace or simply never developed these attributes. Companies often were left with a passive workforce and a rift between workers and management that was spanned only by the occasional use of informal (interpersonal) mentoring—by a supervisor or technical or professional person who decided to help a (usually) younger or less-experienced subordinate. Today, companies that rely on the Machine-Age model often face these same problems.

- *A tendency to characterize people by the work they do.* Because of this myopic perception, companies that embrace the Machine-Age model often fail to explore the many facets of each employee's personality, aspirations, talents, and experience.

Clearly, today's organizations need employee involvement, contribution, and commitment—elements that are hardly brought out by an outmoded, passive form of mentoring.

A DIFFERENT WAY

The civilian personnel office of the U.S. Coast Guard is developing and testing an advanced Information Age form of mentoring that will be available to nearly 40,000 personnel (civilian and military alike). This challenge is complicated by the reality that most units are highly specialized; many are in remote locations—from Alaska to the Caribbean, and from Hawaii to Maine. Some units consist of only a handful of people; others are quite large. Their missions range from drug interdiction to marine safety, and from environmental cleanup services to ship inspection.

The personnel office plans to use mentoring for improving the quality of worklife, training in specialized technical skills, and adapting its operations to take advantage of rapidly developing workforce diversity. The effort will include:

- Mentor training to enable a person to operate across the entire mentor spectrum, to meet short-term situational needs, and to work within the context of both informal and formal mentor relationships.

- Mentee training that helps the learner build a "partnering" relationship with a mentor, take greater responsibility for self-development, and make more effective use of what a mentor can offer.

- A highly flexible voluntary system of mentoring whereby mentors and mentees decide if they can or should work together.

- A formal system that is non-burdensome, non-bureaucratic, and virtually self-managed; a mentoring coordinator identifies appropriate matches and leaves the task of forming the relationship up to the potential participants.

- An electronic bulletin board system whereby mentees list their needs and mentors list their skills as a way of matching participants.

- An electronic mailbox system so that a specialist in Nome, Alaska, can mentor a novice in Miami, Florida.

- Supplementary mentoring as the need arises by phone and fax.

- An open system that allows for multiple mentors or mentees, or for a given individual to serve as a mentor or mentee, or both, as the situation warrants.

The office also loans related training videos and provides sample workbooks to units that request them. The workbooks can be used for self-study or by discussion groups to enhance mentor/mentee skills. This sharing of information enables even small, remote units to engage in mentoring. As the system expands, it will create a greater market for ideas and knowledge.

The new commandant, Admiral Robert Kramek, has stated that he expects all flag officers and senior executive service personnel to mentor at least three persons, and that the mentoring must include women and minorities. In time it is likely that mentoring will become a way of life in the Coast Guard.

A major electronics manufacturer engineered a similar program at their corporate headquarters location. Recognizing that new corporate hires and personnel transferred from other divisions had to adapt quickly to the fast-paced corporate culture, a diverse task force, spearheaded by the human resources manager, created an advanced two-pronged mentoring program:

A Formal Program that matches inside mentors with newcomers to bring their mentees to full participation and assimilation as quickly as possible.

Informal Mentor/Mentee Training provided on an ongoing basis so that any employee can participate in mentoring relationships as needs and inclinations dictate.

This approach is characterized by:

Immediate Application—The formal program aims at achieving specific organizational results now, as well as laying the relationship foundations for more comprehensive and long-term mentee developmental benefits.

Efficient Information Flow—The process is focused on the efficient sharing and transfer of skills and information on best practices in a value-added context.

Its Democratic Nature—By offering informal mentor/mentee training in "lunch bag seminars," virtually every employee could, in time, engage in an effective mentoring relationship.

Egalitarianism—Pairing of mentors and mentees on meeting knowledge needs rather than on relative rank and hierarchy.

Being Mentee-Driven—A switch from what the mentor can give to what the mentee needs has led to an increasing emphasis on mentee performance, more comprehensive mentor/mentee training, and a deemphasis on "copy cat" learning.

A Partnership—The relationship is based on a mutually developed agreement and terminates when the mentee's learning or performance objectives are met, unless a new or modified agreement is formulated.

Mutuality—The program provides for a no-fault divorce if either partner is not satisfied with what is going on between them.

In the balance of this briefing, we will explore how mentoring can be used to each organization's and employee's advantage, and where this management art appears to be heading. We will, at times, pay respect to the older forms of mentoring by offering advice on how these programs can be more effective. But this briefing is devoted, unabashedly, to promoting the new, Information-Age mentoring.

1

Why the Renewed Interest in Mentoring?

Mentoring is one of the oldest forms of human development. Archaeologists and anthropologists trace its origins back to the Stone Age, when especially talented flint knappers, healers, cave artists, and shamans instructed younger people in the arts and knowledge needed to perpetuate their skills, thus laying the foundations for the earliest civilizations. Mentoring cannot be considered a fad or an inconsequential activity.

Thousands of years later, Homer, in the pages of *The Odyssey*, assigned the name Mentor to this type of caring and beneficent individual, and people began to recognize the special characteristics of Mentor in individuals they had known. In time, the term *mentor* came to refer to a person who served as trusted friend, guide, teacher, adviser, and helper to another. Today, one definition of mentoring is:

> A developmental, caring, sharing, and helping relationship where one person invests time, know-how, and effort in enhancing another person's growth, knowledge, and skills, and responds to critical needs in the life of that person in ways that prepare the individual for greater productivity or achievement in the future.

More specifically, a mentor is described as:

> . . . anyone who has a beneficial life- or style-altering effect on another person, generally as a result of personal one-on-one contact; one who offers knowledge, insight, perspective, or wisdom that is helpful to another person in a relationship which goes beyond duty or obligation.

In some ways, the latter definition is more significant, since it stresses the importance of *voluntary action,* one of the most distinguishing characteristics of mentoring.

Mentoring is gaining renewed attention today in business, government, and other institutional environments for a number of reasons. Specifically, it is being used to achieve the following goals:

1. To Advance the Interests of Special Groups and Populations

Previous to the last decade, organizations largely used mentoring to help members of select groups rise in the organization. Today, other groups of employees who were not so favored in the past have, in effect, declared, "We want in." Women, as well as members of racial, ethnic, and other definable groups, have seized upon mentoring as a way to help themselves gain advantages equivalent to those of the "old boy network."

Whereas "Machine-Age" mentoring programs tended to develop managers and executives who looked, thought, and acted as their elders did, new mentoring programs increasingly draw out the diverse characteristics of individuals. These new programs are often initiated not by the organization's leaders, but by the group members themselves. Today's forward-thinking human resources executives support these group efforts. They recognize that women's efforts to break through the glass ceiling and organizational efforts to achieve workplace fairness, workforce diversity, and employee development are intertwined.

Consider, for example, the program being developed by Harrah's Casinos. Harrah's will be opening a new facility (in 1995) adjacent to the French Quarter (Canal Street) in New Orleans. As at other Harrah's facilities, management is exploring mentoring as a way to expand employee opportunities, particularly for less experienced personnel.

The company is particularly interested in ensuring that it has an avenue to help minorities and women move into supervisory positions. Besides being concerned with Parish regulations relating to equal opportunity, Harrah's wants to establish an internship that includes mentoring. This program will focus on helping people upgrade skills as well as cross over into operations positions, such as slot supervision, slot repairs, or food and beverage service.

Often, programs that are developed initially to meet the needs of special groups expand to include a broader range of participants, as the box on page 16 indicates.

2. To Conserve and Transfer Special Know-How

Technical mentoring, as it is often regarded, is frequently used to bring new technical hires up to speed in a short time. This kind of mentoring also enhances product knowledge and smoothes the edges on newly formed teams. It provides an efficient adjunct to apprenticeship and certification training.

Richard Jaffason, executive director of the National Certification Commission in Chevy Chase, Maryland, underscores the broader role that mentoring plays in a certification process. As Jaffason points out, "Today, a waste-water plant operator, a process engineer at a food or drug production facility, or a control operator at a hazardous chemical facility must be far more than a competent technician. [These individuals] cannot afford gaps in their understanding of the relationship between what their jobs entail and the broader environment in which their work is performed." Jaffason points out that a technician's actions can have potential impacts on a host of people, places, and things, which means that certification must include devel-

The Bank of Montreal

Mentoring is part of the Bank of Montreal's new endeavor to foster workplace equality. This Canadian organization, a leader in financial services, is recognized as having some of the most comprehensive and visible attempts to promote women.

Between 1991 and 1992, the percentage of women promoted into executive ranks at the bank climbed from 29 to 54 percent, promotions into senior management from 20 to 38 percent, and promotions into middle management from 43 to 57 percent. Although women are numerous in the banking industry, they are scarce in senior management and executive ranks. The marked success of the Bank of Montreal's programs justified its place as one of the three companies to win the 1994 Catalyst Award. (Catalyst is an organization that seeks to effectively dismantle the glass ceiling for women.)

In 1990, the Bank of Montreal found some surprising statistics: 75 percent of the bank's 34,000 employees were women, but only 9 percent of these women were executives. An employee survey, launched by the bank's Task Force on the Advancement of Women, identified a need for mentoring. Johanne Totta, vice president of workplace equality, took on the task of studying what other companies were doing with mentoring. "Quite frankly," she concluded, "we saw a lot of failure out there. So we are not forcing mentoring and are not forcing pairing."

The bank's program allows the senior managers (the mentees) to list up to three executives they would like to have as mentors. The managers are then paired with one of their three choices. Another unique feature is that the executives mentor both female and male managers, thus extending the program beyond its original purpose.

Initially, the executives wanted only high-potentials (employees who had done well in their performance appraisals) to be mentored. Eventually, they realized the benefits of mentoring all levels of employees.—*Mira Son, Editorial Assistant* oping "a sense of social responsibility." This is where mentoring comes into play. "Mentoring offers special counseling and a variety of forms of support. It aims at developing a well-rounded individual with balanced judgment, broad perspectives, and even a kind of wisdom."

Many companies first began to recognize (in many cases, belatedly) the need to transfer special organization-specific knowledge during the 1980s, when precipitous downsizings produced substantial losses in organizational memory and know-how. More recently, many of those organizations offering early retirement incentives discovered that much expertise goes out the window with those who depart. And, in some cases, the companies have had to hire individuals back on a temporary basis.

In an effort to identify effective approaches to downsizing, Michael Hitt and his colleagues at Texas A&M University interviewed executives at 65 companies that had recently undergone large-scale reductions in force. Executives at firms that had managed a relatively smooth transition often identified mentoring as one of several helpful initiatives. These companies maintained mentoring programs prior to and during the actual layoffs. The programs aimed at developing new leadership as well as retaining technical knowledge.

3. To Encourage Mentee Contribution

In the past, mentees were almost never seriously trained to take an active role in a mentoring relationship. Junior personnel were commonly paired with very senior people, and were treated as "empty vessels" waiting to be filled. Today, however, the emphasis on employee participation, worker empowerment, and team decision making belies the notion that lower level employees have little or nothing to contribute. Consequently, mentees today are increasingly being trained to make the most of being mentored, and to participate as a partner in their own development.

As these trends indicate, today's mentor-mentee team is

more focused on mentee performance and more proactive in contributing to technical and organizational problem solving than ever before. Central to today's mentoring efforts is the goal of greater mentee involvement, responsibility, and investment. This attitude encourages the rapid transfer of technical know-how, creative ideas, and special perspectives, and it leads the mentees to more readily accept and use all offered information, as well as to contribute their own ideas and know-how.

4. To Bring Employees Together in a New Social Environment

The shift from management to leadership, the growing employee insistence on participation in decision making, and the increasing importance of quality-of-worklife and workforce diversity issues have created a new social context within organizations. Although various writers and researchers have studied this new social context, we have yet to see an overall conceptual paradigm emerge.

Mentoring, one element within this new social context, appears to liberate the innate sense of altruism in individuals, *unless that altruism has been stunted.* Some people are unwilling to share their knowledge, skills, and know-how, fearing the recipient will use it to get *their* jobs, or to move ahead of them. Others are angry because they had to struggle to gain their own competence and position, and would just as soon let others go through the same difficulty (since they can seldom get even with the person or people who caused them such grief). And still others are so focused on achieving their own goals that they believe helping others would interfere. However, in virtually every organization, group, or community, a great many unsung heroes are happily helping others.

Mentoring tends to bring individuals together, often for a very long time. It helps individuals get to know one another more closely than in many other types of associations. The prevalence of helping, so characteristic of mentoring, often creates goodwill and even produces friendships between the two individuals. In this way, mentoring is an effective way for organizations to encourage people to derive good feelings about their work, their workmates, and their workplaces.

Current mentoring practices often provide for individuals to have multiple mentors over time, with each one chosen to meet a specific need. For example, one mentor may help an individual master a particular technical field, another may enable that same person to assume a supervisory role, and a third may help him or her learn to manage large projects or programs. As people's lives lengthen and more individuals launch two or three careers (sometimes more) during their lives, the number of mentors and/or mentees a person has is likely to increase. Thus, in time mentoring can help us to create a great many helping relationships and consequently a more civil and caring workplace.

5. To Help Individuals Reach Their Full Potential

It takes a strong and able workforce to create a strong and able organization. On-the-job training and workshops of various sorts can provide employees with most of the knowledge and skills they need to get their jobs done. Tutoring and coaching by supervisors and technical personnel can round off this development.

But individuals often sense that there is another, more personal dimension that is not being addressed effectively. These individuals are vaguely aware that something in the way they work or relate to others is thwarting their development— but they cannot define the problem or attack it successfully.

One person many fear speaking up in a crowd; another may be driven by an inner anger; another may be so competitive that he cannot adjust to a team program. Still another may not know how to dress appropriately, or how to plan a part-time college program. A mentor may not be able to solve all such problems (nor should he or she be expected to), but the mentor can listen to the problem, assist in clarifying the issues, help the employee identify a solution, and encourage the mentee's new behavior.

The closeness that mentors and mentees are able to develop often permits a type of candor and caring assistance that overcomes past roadblocks and opens new vistas. Many executives and managers recognize that mentoring is an idea whose time has come—again.

6. To Enhance Competitive Position

Bottom line considerations do not yet seem to be the primary driving force behind the use of mentoring within organizations. This seems strange, in one respect, since mentoring is always purposeful and aims at enabling people to improve their performances, often in a variety of productive ways.

Yet, when people speak of their mentors and of the mentoring received, they frequently discuss life- or style-altering effects. They talk about how mentoring improved their skills, gave them insider knowledge and/or made them a more effective person. There exists a general recognition that mentoring pays off through improved personal productivity, better decision making, and enhanced job performance. Cumulatively, these things could only help to reflect favorably on the bottom line.

However, two aspects of mentoring make it difficult for us to assign specific weight or substance to the development that takes place.

Aspect 1. Mentoring is such a personal thing, varying in effect so greatly from person to person, that it is difficult to evaluate the learning progress. The mentor tries to discover the extent of the mentee's knowledge, skills, and abilities and then fill in the gaps with mentor-specific (but also unique) forms of help. Consequently, there is no standardized test to measure or prove the effectiveness of a mentoring relationship.

Mentors who have helped numerous mentees report that every relationship is unique. Mentee needs are as diverse as the human beings who present themselves, and the art of the mentor shapes their development in equally unique ways. Mentoring is a treacherous area for those who love to keep scorecards.

Aspect 2. The quiet mastery of complex and interrelated behaviors—the honing and polishing of leadership skills, for example—takes considerable time. Since there are no easily discernible increments to learning, the learner's development may be hidden from view until he or she "goes on stage" or "takes command." What the audience sees, at that moment, appears to be a "whole performance" and a natural outpouring of ability, rather than an act that was long in crafting. The bottom line of that performance is seldom traced to its origins.

We, as Americans, are not known for investing in long-term results. Yet, years may pass between the time a bit of wisdom is passed from mentor to mentee and the occasion for its use arises.

Typically, mentors add to their mentees' data base and response capabilities, arming them with the ammunition needed for future struggles. Since such payoffs are in the indefinite future, there is no practical way to factor them into the bottom line. And when these events happen, there will be no way to credit them appropriately. We need to take these gains on faith—very much as we do with our investment in educating our young. We know we couldn't maintain our society if we didn't do so, yet we can't add those effects to our current bottom line.

The final scene of Homer's mentoring saga is instructive. Mentor supplies Telemachus, now grown, with the weapons this warrior prince and his father, Odysseus, need to battle the would-be usurpers of the throne of Ithaca. Even the gods of ancient Greece had not foreseen this ultimate consequence of Mentor's help.

7. To Develop a More Civil Society

The Training & Development Corporation, a not-for-profit organization headquartered in Bucksport, Maine, operates a summer employment program in which disadvantaged young people (ages 14 to 21) work for ten weeks in a local company. Supported by the U.S. Department of Labor, the program matches each youth with a volunteer supervisor. But to participate, supervisors must complete a mentoring workshop that trains them in how to reach young people who have been unsuccessful in both school and prior job assignments. To date, the program has produced highly rewarding experiences for the supervisor-mentors. And many of the young participants report a new-found confidence in themselves—and a new hope for the future.

Actually, this type of program is far from unique. Tens of thousands of volunteer mentors are working in their communities, schools, and religious institutions to help young people live better lives, benefit from more varied options, and gain success in critical "gateway" activities. Volunteers in successful "stay in school" type programs help high school students gain self-esteem, see themselves as achievers rather than failures, and expand their horizons to include previously unthinkable possibilities. Among these community mentors are FBI field agents, Coast Guard captains, and small businesspeople, as well as carpenters, janitors, and retired school teachers who care about what happens to young people. The key here, however, is that many of these programs are employer sponsored or encouraged.

But regardless of their sponsorship, several important themes tie these programs together:

- They are one-on-one and very personal;
- They encourage listening, caring, and other forms of involvement between mentors and mentees; and
- They provide a cumulative beneficial effect on mentees that counteracts many of the negative forces at work in society.

It's clear that many types of mentoring are developing, and the investment in others that mentors are making is increasing.

As a result, the varied uses of mentoring have piqued the interest and imagination of individuals who see opportunity for personal and organizational gain through the use of this extraordinary form of human development.

2

What Makes Mentoring Different and Special?

Mentoring can be a catalyst, a facilitator, a linking device, or even an organizational neural network. It can be an intellectual supplement, an employee exercise plan, and a performance builder.

But mostly, mentoring can be a tool for broadening the vision and capability of virtually every employee.

In an increasing number of organizations, mentoring has become a way to knit the organization together; to extend the organization's impact beyond the corporate walls to society at large; and to create a healthier, more prosperous business world. In fact, some see mentoring as a highly effective strategy for helping individuals adjust to the rapid changes occurring in their personal lives, their organizations, and society as a whole.

Because organizations tend to institute mentoring formally, many people read its arrival in terms of their past experience with similar efforts—that is, as "just another program." Contrary to these perceptions, mentoring is a form of one-on-one training and development; it is one of the three basic ways that we teach and learn. (See Exhibit 2-1.)

Exhibit 2-1. Basic Types of Learning.

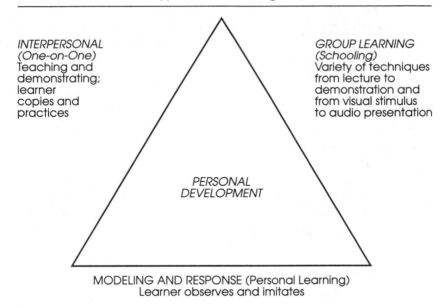

INTERPERSONAL
(One-on-One)
Teaching and
demonstrating;
learner
copies and
practices

GROUP LEARNING
(Schooling)
Variety of techniques
from lecture to
demonstration and
from visual stimulus
to audio presentation

PERSONAL
DEVELOPMENT

MODELING AND RESPONSE (Personal Learning)
Learner observes and imitates

Let's look at these three basic types of learning.

1. Modeling and Response. This, the most basic form of teaching and learning, occurs almost from the time we are born. Our parents communicate with us repetitively, and eventually we learn to mimic their behavior. In time, each of their behaviors enters our own repertoire of behaviors. As we develop, this kind of modeling becomes more abstract. For example, by watching a movie or reading a book, we learn complex ways to behave—e.g., we model styles of leadership based on a fictional or historical hero.

2. Interpersonal (One-on-One) Training and Development. This form of conscious human development probably began when groups of people had something—an art or a bit of science or technology—they wanted to pass on to talented, gifted, or, perhaps, just interested individuals. This, they believed, would preserve that knowledge or skill for the benefit of the group or tribe.

3. Group Learning (Schooling). Group teaching and learning is a response to the economics of need and the availability of knowledge or skills that can be effectively communicated to many others. While this form of group development is also quite old (it can be traced back, at least, to the emergence of hunting and gathering societies), it endures because it provides social interaction and cross learning in addition to the transfer of large amounts of knowledge and skill. (It will likely never be replaced, completely, by solitary learning in front of a computer screen.)

By taking a closer look at one-on-one forms of learning, we can put mentoring into its proper perspective and begin to answer the question this chapter raises—what, exactly, is it that gives mentoring its special power?

MENTORING ADDS AN EXTRA DIMENSION TO ONE-ON-ONE DEVELOPMENT

A teacher, for example, typically imparts bits and pieces of knowledge or skills one step at a time. He or she then helps the learner link each piece of knowledge to other pieces, until a "unit" of learning is achieved. For example, children learning their "ABCs" are taught one letter at a time, in the correct order, until they can repeat the entire alphabet. Then they put these letters together to form words.

There are five types of one-on-one learning relationships (see Exhibit 2-2), and each involves some form of teaching—i.e., passing on bits of information (and, to a lesser degree, skills) in long chains until a module of learning occurs. There are, however, important differences between these relationships. (A teacher passes on knowledge while a coach, for example, works on performance of the individual, shaping various behaviors and actions into a more productive whole.)

1. Teaching. A teacher seldom *just* lectures—especially today. One-on-one interaction abounds in the average classroom, as

Exhibit 2-2. Modes of One-on-One Teaching and Helping.

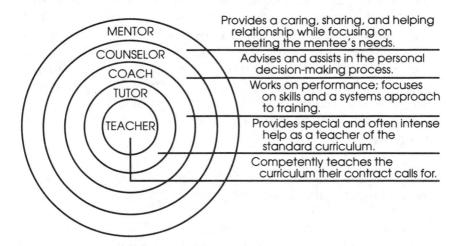

MENTOR — Provides a caring, sharing, and helping relationship while focusing on meeting the mentee's needs.

COUNSELOR — Advises and assists in the personal decision-making process.

COACH — Works on performance; focuses on skills and a systems approach to training.

TUTOR — Provides special and often intense help as a teacher of the standard curriculum.

TEACHER — Competently teaches the curriculum their contract calls for.

when a student asks a question or when the teacher calls upon a student to respond. However, the effect of this teacher-student interaction usually offers learning to the whole class and may even enhance the teacher's awareness, knowledge (by association of a new idea with his or her existing knowledge), or insight.

2. Tutoring. A tutor normally covers the same ground in the same way as a teacher. However, the closeness of the relationship enables the tutor to detect and close gaps in the learner's knowledge, or to address subject matter difficulties the learner is having. Thus, the tutor can respond directly to the learner's needs or even experiment with alternate and more effective ways of communicating with that individual.

3. Coaching. One-on-one coaching (as opposed to team coaching) allows the learner to receive specialized attention whenever a problem occurs. In addition, the coach pays attention to the details of the total "human system," thus synchronizing all parts of the individual who is learning the task. For example, in helping someone make an artful presentation, the coach attempts to guide the presenter in crafting a display of him- or herself as well as of the material, and thus achieve the desired effect.

4. *Counseling*. Within organizations, counseling is often seen as a means of improving individual behavior or performance. Used ineptly, i.e., as an effort to force certain behavior, it can evoke employee coping mechanisms and cause the problem to go underground rather than be resolved. To use counseling constructively, the counselor must focus on helping the individual become successful and productive in the workplace. When used this way, counseling, in most situations, can produce harmony between the interests of the individual and those of the organization.

5. *Mentoring*. The distinctive aspect of mentoring is that it focuses almost entirely on meeting the needs of the mentee. The mentor devotes him- or herself to this unselfish effort.

Actually, a teacher (and members of other professions as well) may operate in any of the five roles defined in Exhibit 2-2. One teacher may just teach. Another may also tutor or coach a given student. Some may counsel . . . and a few may mentor. Mentoring is a special relationship, and it requires its own set of attitudes, values, and behaviors.

MENTORING: AN EXCEPTIONAL EXPERIENCE

Consider the notion of "good, better, best" in the context of teachers you have had. It is likely that during your formal education, you had between 15 and 50 teachers. It is also likely that the majority of these teachers were "good" teachers: They taught their subjects competently, followed the curriculum, and you learned at least enough to move on to the next grade or course level. Teachers like these did their duty and earned their pay. But the experience of being in their class is probably difficult to remember clearly.

You also had some teachers who offered you more than competence. These "better" teachers invested more in mastering the material and excelling in their presentation of it. They were the teachers who made their subjects come alive. Their classrooms crackled with energy. They challenged their students, and they created imaginings their students had never envisioned before. These teachers were, in essence, responding to their own inner drive to do the best possible job they could. While this is certainly a valuable and worthy motivation, it's a self-oriented one, nevertheless.

However, if you were especially fortunate, you had one or more teachers who touched your life and influenced it for the better. Such teachers went beyond the curriculum or their teaching obligations; they invested time, energy, imagination, and effort in helping you make a life- or style-altering change. These individuals are the people we fondly remember as mentors. These were our *best* teachers because they reached beyond their material and "touched" us.

Mentors come in all styles and types. They may be patient listeners who permit us to ventilate the strong feelings (anger, fear, or grief) that are keeping us stuck in place; they may be stern taskmasters who hold us to the highest standards of performance we are capable of (even when we do not think we are capable of them); they may be patient encouragers who help us move toward some goal of our own. Or, they may be technical or professional people who teach us the ropes, drawing out skills we didn't know we had (or we only vaguely recognized) and lighting a spark within us that causes us to aspire to professional performance. Yet all of these types of mentors voluntarily make an investment in us that goes beyond their duties and obligations.

The life- or style-altering effects of the mentor may occur so slowly and subtly that neither mentor nor mentee is fully aware of the change. The mentor is simply doing what he or she likes to do, wanting only to help the mentee. And the mentee is simply participating in a change process that may take years (and, possibly, additional mentors) to complete.

At the same time, both mentor and mentee usually gain deeply felt satisfaction from even a short-term mentoring relationship. The "endorsements," pages 30 and 31, are represen-

An Exceptional Experience for Mentees

The following comments come from individuals who partici-
pated in a formal six-month mentoring program.

• "I never dreamed that I could learn so much in so little
time. His insights into the nature of the organization, how it
works and what it rewards, will, I'm sure, make an enormous
difference in my career. But, it is our friendship that I will value
the most."

• "When I came to really know her, I knew I'd not feel
alone again as long as there were people like her in the
organization. I've learned to trust more and to take charge of
my own future through her help."

• "I never dreamed that a highly successful executive
could care so much about what would happen to me. I hope I
can repay him by making good use of all those special insights
he provided. All I could say was, 'Thanks for everything!' It
didn't seem like enough."

• "I'm contributing much more to our work team effort than
I was just six months ago. I've been able to turn my whole
attitude around. I'd give him credit for that but he wouldn't
accept it. He'd say I did it, he only helped, but without that
help I doubt if I'd have made it. The mentoring experience has
changed my life for the better."

• "Now that I know what mentoring is, I plan to do voluntary
mentoring in our community. Helping young people will help
pay back what I've gained. Thanks!"

tative of the thousands of comments I have received from
individuals who have had the experience.

MENTORS HELP—BUT MENTEES *DO!*

If a mentor gives of him- or herself, the mentee will almost
certainly benefit. Virtually everyone can use encouragement,

An Exceptional Experience for Mentors

Mentors also report interesting and sometimes surprising responses to their mentoring experiences.

- "Mentoring has added another dimension to my leadership skills. Going the extra mile was just an interesting expression until I was trained to function as a mentor."
- "I never dreamed how much I knew that was special to me until I began to mentor my technical team members. Things I had observed or reasoned out, but never wrote down, kept coming back to me as their needs kept popping up."
- "During training, getting in touch with prior mentoring experiences revealed to me how many valuable things I had gained from informal mentoring experiences I've had, and how long their effect has lasted—decades in some cases."
- "When I help my mentee achieve something special and important to them, I feel I've made a powerful investment in our organization's most valuable asset—its people."
- "Becoming a mentor helped me to stop thinking of my work group as just a group. The very personal one-on-one investment in another person helped me to see each one as an individual and then our team as a synergy of harmonies, and as cooperative, unique individuals. I like this."
- "Cross-cultural and cross-gender mentoring experiences have opened my eyes, really opened them, to the fresh perspectives, creativity, and dynamic potential inherent in tapping into differences in the work groups. . . . This is a refreshing change."

help, guidance, information, ideas, new options, and opportunities from time to time. If a mentor notices that an individual has a need, a desire, a hope, an aspiration, a talent, or even a vague discomfort with him- or herself, there may be a mentoring opportunity.

We should also recognize that mentoring is seldom a full-time job. If we look at Exhibit 2-2 again, we can see that a teacher will spend most of his or her time teaching, and may also spend time tutoring students who are having trouble with the subject matter. The same teacher may also coach a gifted student for a competitive examination, or counsel him or her about a personal problem. If any of these types of helping go on long enough or are intense enough to make a significant difference in a person's life, that teacher, tutor, coach, or counselor may also become that person's mentor. Mentoring may take place during odd moments when the other students are working on a project, or after school hours. But regardless of when it takes place, mentoring is a special form of help that makes a lasting difference.

MENTORING: A VOLUNTARY ACTIVITY

It has been said that you can't hire a mentor. The reason is that the mentor's expectation of compensation could contaminate the relationship. After all, it is difficult to focus exclusively on the needs of the mentee when one's income is involved.

Mentoring adds an extra or special dimension to a helping relationship; one that tends to be unconditional and about as pure as anything in human affairs can be. But it is precisely because both participants are free from the burden of duty and obligation that their imaginations can soar. The mentor experiences the unalloyed joy of seeing a friend succeed at his or her chosen goal, and the mentee experiences the joy of achieving success!

3

Mentoring: A Program or a Way of Life?

Many organizations now view mentoring as a highly flexible, variable, and comprehensive way of developing each employee's productive capabilities. The potential of mentoring can be seen in the spectrum of mentoring behaviors displayed in Exhibit 3-1. Mentoring is increasingly being perceived as:

• A flexible developmental art potentially helpful to *every* member of the workforce.

• A source of varied opportunities if mentors are trained in using the whole spectrum of mentoring behaviors.

• A way to enhance the flow of valuable information, skills, insights, and ideas among associates throughout the organization, via any media and in any direction (even from outside the organization, when appropriate).

• A mentee-driven strategy; more workers are taking charge of their own development, aware of the help available, and are seeking out situational, informal, and formal mentor training as their needs become more explicit.

• A source of flexible and interchangeable roles to adopt, since individuals can assume the mentee or mentor role as their needs and abilities dictate for any given situation (this is in contrast to the traditional mentor/protege concept, which implies only a "top down" relationship).

• A source of opportunities for diverse supplemental growth experiences, since mentors and mentees can network to maximum effect.

• A results-centered (as opposed to process-centered) partnership.

This list is not intended to suggest that the old type of mentoring is disappearing; it's merely designed to show that the number of mentoring options available is growing. Nevertheless, anyone hoping to achieve the promise of mentoring must recognize three additional points:

1. Mentoring is measured by the effect it has on the mentee, now and/or in the future. One mentor may help an individual turn a corner in his or her life, so that from that moment forward the person is different and behaves differently. Another may help that person master the skills needed to open new doors, build a successful career, live a fuller, more satisfying life, and/or contribute to others more effectively.

2. The benefits of mentoring are not a straight function of the time invested. As an art form, mentoring may produce a dramatic change in a moment, or may take years of effort to produce a desired outcome. A formal mentoring program, in which mentor and mentee are paired for months, may focus on teaching the basics of a business operation, as the mentor/mentee agreement requires. This may produce specific and highly useful results, even though little time is actually spent mentoring in the full sense of the word. The learner's ability to use those basics in more skillful and creative ways may not come until years later. (In organizationally sponsored formal mentoring programs, mentor and mentee typically schedule meetings for one hour or less a week on or off organizational time.)

Exhibit 3-1. Spectrum of mentor interactions.

SITUATIONAL RESPONSES	INFORMAL RELATIONSHIP	FORMAL PROGRAM OR TRADITION
Isolated, specific acts by mentor to meet current mentee needs	Interpersonal agreement or understanding for mentor to help mentee—usually in specific areas	Structured program to meet organizational (or societal) goals

3. Mentee involvement must be high. Remember the axiom, Mentors help—Mentees do! Actually, it's not quite that one-sided. The mentor may offer something of value, but the mentee may simply be unable to make much use of that help at that particular point in time. This is why empowerment training, as well as a mentee's own efforts to overcome a tendency toward passivity, are critical to mentee development. At the same time, mentors may see the mentee's inability to move forward as a problem to be solved—and openly help the mentee confront that problem. This may lead them to cooperatively devise greater, more imaginative efforts.

TYPES OF MENTORING

Exhibit 3-2 illustrates the characteristics of the three primary types of mentoring: situational, informal, and formal. The three types of mentoring blend with one another. For example, formal mentoring programs can range from tight, bureaucratically controlled operations at the extreme right of the spectrum shown in Exhibit 3-1 to loose associations, where the only formal aspect is that the partners agree to meet weekly or decide upon one or more objectives within a general time frame.

1. Situational Mentoring. Some of the most powerful mentoring experiences occur in short bursts, when an individual provides the right information or ideas at the right moment in another person's life. The mentor may simply be responding to the mentee's need out of a "helping habit," without realizing the impact her or his words are having. In fact, neither party may recognize the activity as mentoring. However, the incident may produce a significant life- or style-altering effect on the other person.

Hoosiers, the film portraying the career of Norman Dale, illustrates situational mentoring. The film takes place in 1951, in the tiny town of Hickory, Indiana—"a place that takes its

Exhibit 3-2. Characteristics of different types of mentoring.

SITUATIONAL MENTORING ACTS

Tend to be:

- Short, isolated episodes
- Spontaneous, "off-the-cuff" interventions
- Seemingly random
- Often casual
- Creative and innovative

Are generally characterized by being:

- Responsive to current needs of mentee and/or present situation
- A mentor-initiated intervention
- "One time" events
- The mentee's responsibility to recognize and use lessons offered
- Unclear as to results at time of incident

May include:

- Sharp, beneficial life- or style-altering effects on mentee
- Increased sensitivity of mentee to *opportunities*
- A network of mentors to be called upon as needed
- Later assessment of results by mentee

INFORMAL MENTORING RELATIONSHIPS

Tend to be:

- Voluntary
- Very personal
- Very responsive to mentee needs
- Loosely structured
- Flexible

Are generally characterized by being:

- Mentor-driven by his or her caring, sharing, and helping
- A mutual acceptance of roles (giver-receiver)
- A path to developing deep mutual respect and friendship
- Dependent on mentor's competence, knowledge, skills, and abilities

Exhibit 3-2. Continued.

May include:

- Mentee-revealed needs
- Periodic assessment of results by participants
- Team mentoring, but with emphasis on intense one-on-one interaction during team activity
- Mentor having more than a one-role relationship with mentee—i.e., as a supervisor, parent, or friend

FORMAL MENTORING PROGRAMS

Tend to be:

- Measurably productive and long term
- The source of a developing relationship—friendship
- Systematic and structured
- Institutionalized and ongoing
- Traditional

Are generally characterized by being:

- Driven by organizational needs
- Focused on achieving organizational or subunit goals
- A method for matching mentors with (or assigned to) mentees
- Of fixed duration and based on goal achievement
- Organizationally sponsored or sanctioned

May include:

- Monitoring of program activities
- Measurement of program results, as with organizational change or the advancement of specific groups of mentees
- A focus on goals of a special group
- Specially designed organizational interventions

---

basketball as seriously as its religion." Dale becomes coach of Hickory High's eight-man hoop squad and leads them to win the state championship in one season. One of the film's clearest portrayals of Dale's mentoring comes when this rural team, used to playing in small-town high school gyms, enters the huge stadium where they are to vie in the playoffs. The awe on the players faces is overwhelming. Dale takes a tape measure from his pocket and has the players measure the hoop distances. He then announces that the dimensions are the same as in their gym back in Hickory, thus, demystifying the situation. The presence of the tape measure was no accident, of course, and the lessons learned by the players went far beyond the obvious ones.

Such an event may produce a turning point in a person's career—although the mentee may not perceive it as a mentoring experience until many years later.

The value of such a casual transfer of information or ideas depends largely on how well the mentee accepts and uses the information. If the information offered fits the mentee's needs, the impact can be substantial. Consider the following questions, based on your own life experience.

- Who provided you with an "Aha!" experience that enabled you to grasp the significance of something important—something that had, up until then, eluded you?
- Who provided you with a "quotable quote" that illuminated the essence of something and suddenly had great meaning for you, so that you still repeat it—even to others?
- Who helped you discover an ability or talent that had been previously dormant?

When groups of prospective mentors have been asked these three questions, virtually all of them can identify one or more significant incidents that influenced their lives.

2. Informal Mentoring Relationships. Informal mentoring is probably the most common type of mentoring and may last from a few weeks to a lifetime. Such informal mentoring may lead to friendships that include occasional mentoring experiences as well.

Flexible, loosely structured, informal relationships are usually mentor initiated or driven, in that the mentor voluntarily shares whatever expertise or special insights he or she possesses when another person appears to have a need for such help. While each partner usually has a clearly defined role (giver versus receiver), a peer relationship may develop in which the two switch roles, depending on who needs help at a given time.

When a teacher, tutor, coach, or counselor goes beyond his or her obligations or narrow self-interest, the informal mentoring role often comes into play. This "above and beyond" concept is at the core of much biography and literature (such as many sports epics), in which the helping agent breaks free from the hold of his or her own job obligations and potential gain, and, instead, does what is best for the mentee. Such individuals are mentors in the full sense of the word.

If you can identify one or more people who were mentors in your life, chances are good that the relationship fit the definition of "informal mentoring." In other words, the relationship carried beyond situational incidents but was not formalized beyond the help given to you—there was no stated agreement, official sanction, or established time frame.

Some organizations train *all* of their employees to mentor one another informally as needs arise. Surveys in such companies indicate:

- A substantial increase (often 200 to 300 percent) in the number of informal mentoring relationships.
- A much higher incidence of situational mentoring reported by both mentors and mentees. (It was difficult, however, to obtain any statistics comparing the amount of situational mentoring that occurred before training and after training, since these episodes were considered "incidental.")
- A far greater awareness of the availability of mentors and of the needs of others for mentoring (individuals were more sensitive to nonexplicit verbal and nonverbal pleas for assistance and to other indications that an associate might have a problem).

- A more effective response to individuals who needed help, since employees were trained to avoid certain non-productive behaviors and to use more effective techniques.

Many organizations offer training in informal mentoring to those not engaged in an employer-sanctioned formal program.

3. Formal mentoring programs. At the extreme right of the spectrum in Exhibit 3-1, the goals of mentoring tend to be focused narrowly, so that mentoring programs are considered fit for extensive planning, measurement, and evaluation. By contrast, at the point where the formal and informal models meet, "programs" are virtually self-managed by the mentor and mentee, and are driven by a mutually developed set of objectives. Typically, after employees are trained in both how to mentor and how to be an effective mentee, a mentoring coordinator will determine who in the organization wants to learn or develop skills, and who has the appropriate ability to help. He or she will then suggest possible matches, although the participants decide whether or not to work together.

Hence, formal mentoring programs can range from light, inexpensive systems to quite burdensome, expensive, and/or heavily managed activities. Deciding which way to go is not always easy. An organization trying to achieve critical changes in the composition of its workforce may want a more structured approach so that it can measure its progress. On the other hand, an organization that wants to speed problem solving, adapt to rapid change, and become as competitive as possible may opt for the self-managed approach.

Since we will be examining some aspects of formal systems more closely in Chapter 6, a careful examination of the material in Exhibit 3-2 can be useful.

Well-trained mentors and mentees tend to participate in mentoring relationships as a natural and ongoing part of life. Throughout their careers, and sometimes for decades afterwards, the joy and satisfaction that is gained from helping or being helped encourages them to serve in either role as the need and opportunity come into existence. Training mentors and mentees across the entire spectrum of relationships (from situational to formal) enables them to respond more appropriately to the subtleties of a mentee's needs.

4

The Effective Mentor

When Odysseus, King of Ithaca, went to fight in the Trojan War, he entrusted his friend, Mentor, with the education of his son, Telemachus. Mentor's task was to educate, train, and develop the youngster to fulfill his birthright and become king of Ithaca. It can be argued that in a democratic society, people also have a birthright: to become all they can be. And mentors help their mentees move toward fulfilling that birthright.

Mentoring is largely a matter of communicating useful knowledge and skills to someone who wants to learn. That sounds simple enough. But, as anyone familiar with the study of interpersonal communications knows, some communication behaviors can be very productive—others much less so. Examining these behaviors can help us appreciate some of the more subtle aspects of mentoring.

BEHAVIORS TO AVOID

In the past, behaviors such as giving advice, sponsoring, and even "rescuing" (i.e., helping the mentee extricate him- or herself from a potential calamity) might have been considered the essence of mentoring. We now know that these behaviors have a downside—they do little to support a relationship aimed at empowering the learner. Let's take a closer look at the dynamics involved.

Giving Advice

In a mentoring relationship, giving advice can shift responsibility for making a decision from mentee to mentor and curtail personal growth. If the mentee accepts the advice and applies it successfully, the mentor has encouraged dependency. The mentee may return time and again to let the mentor solve his or her problems.

Also, giving advice often carries a subliminal message of, "You are not able to solve your problem . . . let me do it for you." This is why people often resist advice. Rather than be told what to do, they want someone to listen and to support them in their problem solving and decision making endeavors.

Criticizing

Researchers agree that there is no such thing as "constructive criticism," no matter how helpful the giver's intent. By definition, criticism is valuative and judgmental, and therefore, usually perceived as threatening. People tend to resist listening to criticism. And well they should. Our most basic needs, as Maslow defines them, are for survival and security, and criticism threatens these basics. On the other hand, accepting criticism lowers self-esteem and may lead to lower effectiveness.

Mentees often need someone to help them explore where a course of action may lead and to define the gap between *what is* and *what is needed*. Factual information concerning the situation can also be beneficial. Explorations such as these encourage maturity.

Rescuing

Mistakes can lead to growth, assuming the person recognizes the causes of the mistake and uses that information to build better decisions in the future. But let's be truthful: people seldom actually do learn from their mistakes. If they really did, we should encourage them to make more and bigger mistakes, as a "fast track" way of learning.

The issue here is *patterns* of mistakes. If a person's mistakes are driven by a repetitive pattern, such as driving too fast, skirting the edges of the law, or taking excessive risks in other fields, rescuing them from their folly will encourage them to push the envelope further. Parents who constantly rescue their children from the consequences of their acts are the best-known example of this syndrome. They postpone the reckoning—usually disastrous for both when it comes. Ironically, the more the mentor likes a mentee, the more prone he or she may be to rescue the mentee inappropriately.

Sponsoring

In Machine-Age mentoring, it was common for mentors to promote the careers of their proteges. They became press agents for their young charges, often without regard for the protege's relative talent or merit. It was like rooting for the home team, simply because it was theirs.

It is certainly appropriate for a mentor to open a door for a mentee who shows talent. It's also appropriate to inform the mentee of an opportunity or to help her or him prepare for a desired position. But to invest one's own ego in special treatment for a mentee can be the rawest form of favoritism. In a truly competitive arena, talent should win out.

Building Barriers

Mentors sometimes build barriers between themselves and their mentees without intending to, and without being aware that they are doing so. When lower level personnel (interns or even supervisors) find themselves paired with executives, they may find the situation flattering—but also scary. Behavior appropriate for the boardroom can be intimidating for someone who needs a relaxed, friendly environment in which to ask questions or take risks.

Ignoring the *Why*

The essence of training is skill acquisition; its measure is performance. The essence of education is understanding; its measure is new applications. Many mentors are good at knowing what to do and how to do it, and displaying their skill—their own performance is measured by how well they do things. Consequently, they may not invest equal time in educating a person. Education takes longer and is often more complicated.

"Reasons why" are at the center of making sense of things. Children start asking why out of curiosity, but may pursue doing so out of a perverse sense that they can drive their parents (who, in their opinion, should know everything) nuts with enough "whys." Mentors should be able to admit when they don't know the *why* of something. This admission can become the cue for a joint problem-solving exercise. Knowing where to get the answer can be valuable to a mentee who needs to fit knowledge and understanding together in new patterns.

Discounting

People make less of someone, something, or themselves as an unconscious way of dealing with their negative feelings. When we make a mistake, for example, we may put ourselves down ("There I go again. . . . I never do anything right") instead of getting on with making it right.

In mentoring, we might discount a mentee's interest, ability, or willingness to do something we think beneficial ("He should take on this project, but he'll probably mess it up."). A mentor's heightened awareness of his or her hesitations and negative assessments can lead to candid discussion. This is risky—but it's a risk that the mentor needs to be open to.

BEHAVIORS TO PRACTICE

Sometimes it seems easier to get someone to practice a positive behavior than to give up a negative one. For example, we can remind ourselves to listen more intently to the concerns of a mentee—a positive behavior. But stifling the urge to give advice can be much more difficult. The positive behaviors are more rewarding, but the negative ones are familiar and habitual. Below are seven helpful behaviors mentors need to master.

Listening

When a mentee has a concern or problem to discuss, acting as a sounding board may be all that is needed to help this person work through a problem and reach a decision. Careful listening helps mentees achieve two things. It helps them maintain ownership of the problem and their decision about how to solve it, and they gain the pleasure and pride of having solved the problem themselves. By listening, the mentor helps an individual become a more efficient problem solver.

Feedback

When someone explains a problem, the problem description almost always contains both *facts* and *feelings*. If the feelings are negative, they can interfere with a person's problem-solving ability. By giving feedback on the whole message—both the facts and the feelings—you let the other person know that you not only *heard* them, but *understood* them. This makes a mentee feel he or she is not alone with this problem. By gaining perspective on the whole problem (facts and feelings), the mentee is more able to dissipate the negative feeling and get on with the problem solving.

Providing Information and Ideas

Much of what a mentor offers a mentee is in the form of information, personal insight, options, and the like. But *when* we offer this information is important. If a person is locked in the throes of a difficult problem, objective data will seem irrelevant—and it is. However, if the person is able to work through the personal pain, fears, or anger, a time will come where knowledge is helpful. When that time comes, the mentee *is ready for* decision making.

Context Shifting

Individuals have often been trained to imagine themselves living out a certain role or way of life. These self-images may be outdated, limiting, and even inapplicable. Helping a person (without arguing) to see himself/herself in a broader, more self-actualizing, and hopefully more rewarding light can be a great service. This context must jibe with the mentee's nature and abilities (rather than our goals for the mentee). But such a shift in self-image can help individuals maximize their birthright of being all that they can be.

Confrontation

Confronting a mentee's behavior and/or intentions without damaging the mentee's self-image or the relationship is a high art. If the need for confrontation arises, think in terms of giving a clear, non-judgmental description of what you believe the mentee is doing (or intends to do). Describe the consequences you anticipate or observe and express how you feel about the behavior. This should be enough. Hold back any impulse to tell the mentee how to behave or how you would solve the problem. (If we don't give the mentee a directive, there is nothing he or she can argue about or reject.) An artful confrontation gives the mentee something to think about and will usually lead to a decision—one that the mentee will own and hopefully feel good about.

Permission and Encouragement

Before a person can make an important behavior change, he or she may need "psychological permission" from an authority figure—often their mentor. The complexities of human behavior are rooted in early life experiences, parental programming, and notions derived from culture, training, or economic circumstances. Change is not easy. The person may need to explore the sources of certain behavior patterns and evaluate the consequences of keeping the old behaviors or changing. If the person decides that the change would be good, encouragement and support can be critical to his or her success.

Exploring Options

One of the most valuable services a mentor can render is to help a mentee brainstorm or otherwise articulate a variety of options to any decision. These options may be serious or playful, innovative or traditional. Not only does the brainstorming suggest more choices, but it also leads the mentee to more creative variations and a broader perspective on the problem.

WHAT MENTORS DO

If an organization's leaders view mentoring as a way of life rather than as a *program,* then workforce development will be widespread and constant. Mentors trained to use the entire spectrum of mentoring interactions (from situational to formal intervention) can help their associates at all levels whenever the need or opportunity arises, with or without any long-term agreement.

Mentors are people who have special or memorably helpful effects on us and our lives. Typically, mentors make *important* contributions to our:

- Technical competence.
- Character.

- Knowledge of how to get things done in or through the organization.
- Mental and physical health and fitness.
- Understanding of other people and their viewpoints.
- Knowledge of how to behave in unfamiliar social situations.
- Insights into cultural differences.
- Understanding of the historical origins of events and the meaning of trends.
- Creation of an insightful personal data bank.
- Development of values.

Good mentors know the value of their time and recognize the need to get their regular jobs accomplished. Consequently, they often set aside a specific interval for regular meetings with their mentees, knowing it takes time to develop a trusting, productive relationship.

Training mentors to perform the range of mentoring activities productively takes time and investment, but the payoff is reflected in the accomplishment of their mentees and in the fact that the mentor can continue to provide effective mentoring throughout his or her entire career.

"WHAT CAN I CONTRIBUTE?"

Since the older model of top-down (senior to junior) mentoring is giving way to more democratic relationships (including mentoring by peer specialists), many more people are finding the idea of mentoring attractive and personally promising. Nevertheless, many prospective mentors are unsure of whether they have anything of value to offer another person. There are several ways to relieve that concern. First, the potential mentor should try sitting down at the word processor or with a sheet of paper and pen, and (forgoing all modesty) ask him- or herself:

- What am I good at?
- What special experience have I had?

- When have people asked my help?
- What things do I see that other people need to know about?
- What would I enjoy helping someone with the most?

After answering these questions, the individual might choose several items to explore.

MENTOR RELATIONSHIPS

The goals of the mentoring relationship shape the role the mentor will play. Below are three examples of common helping relationships that transcend common workplace associations because of the mentor's focus on the mentee's development. Dozens of other models are possible, depending on the abilities of the mentor and the needs and response of the mentee.

   1. The Role Model.

- Demonstrates appropriate attitudes, behaviors, protocols, and responses; explains why these are appropriate.
- Models effective behavior in his or her daily life and within the organization.
- Inspires the mentee to meet and possibly exceed his or her chosen goals.
- Demonstrates adaptive behaviors and personal learning and growth.
- Supports and encourages mentee learning and constructive development on an ongoing basis.

   2. The Career Counselor. (Note that this is a mentoring role, not the job function of the same name.)

- Acts as a sounding board as the mentee sorts through and reacts to the dilemmas of developing career choices.
- Provides insights into the organization's markets, environ-

ment, culture, and values, as well as to evolving changes in any of these areas.

- Provides access to sources of career information or acts as a reference guide for paths the mentee may choose.
- Shares his or her own personal or business contacts who can help the mentee gain realistic information on his or her options.
- May assist the mentee in planning special career moves, such as lateral moves, assignments on task forces, assignments to special projects, and participation in advanced education and training courses.
- Suggests tactics and strategies for accomplishing work objectives.
- Provides support when the mentee is experiencing stress and uncertainty.
- Offers ideas and information on career development materials, resource contacts, and paths to explore in setting the next stage of the mentee's career path.
- Shares information and ideas on the evolution of careers in a modern context.

3. The Leadership-Coach. (Note: managers today tend to be shifting their focus to leadership rather than just managing.)

- Offers instructive parables, stories, biographical incidents, and legends about leadership and its responsibilities.
- Counsels the "whole person" about values, integrity, and ethical conduct when appropriate.
- Uses the Socratic method of exploring issues with the mentee, discussing where certain paths of conduct will ultimately lead.
- Provides exposure to the values of moral leaders through various media, such as the discussion of films, books, and news stories.
- Helps the mentee recognize outcomes of his or her actions and plans.

- Acts as foil and friend when engaged in discussions of ethical conduct.

Mentor Responsibilities

To ensure productive relationships with their mentees, mentors can take a number of actions, including:

- Setting realistic expectations for the relationship, for mentee achievement, and for their own involvement.
- Being available—to as great an extent as possible—whenever the mentee has a need.
- Maintaining consistent contact with the mentee, to help the relationship develop.
- Listening with empathy.
- Being open minded to the mentee's needs and opinions.
- Providing encouragement.
- Making a conscious effort to build the relationship.
- Following through on commitments.
- Providing emotional support when needed.
- Communicating often, even if only to say "Hello."
- Alerting their mentee to existing or developing opportunities that will help the mentee explore options.
- Sharing information on one's own successes and failures as appropriate.
- Giving and receiving constructive feedback when needed.

THE CONSTANTLY DEVELOPING SELF

In the past, organizational mentors tended to develop themselves slowly, if at all, for the mentoring role. This was because their organizations changed slowly, and since they often passed on well-established principles or facts gleaned from their on-the-job experience, not much personal development was considered necessary.

However, with the advent of the "learning organization"

and the emphasis on continuously developing everyone within it, more and more mentors are struggling to keep up with—let alone keep ahead of—their mentees. This need not be a problem, since a bracing dialogue between mentor and mentee may prove productive and generate mutual learning. If both partners are growing, any concern about who is mentoring and who is being mentored may not be important.

Nevertheless, mentors who make a conscious investment in their own development will tend to become a more valuable resource to others.

5

The Productive Mentee

—The Extra Mile—

The story is told that when the armies of Rome occupied the Holy Land in Biblical times, there was a law that stated that any Roman soldier could impress any Jewish youth to carry his armor for one mile. One such soldier began to tell the youth carrying his armor about the places he had visited, the things he had done, and some of the adventures he had had. As they walked and talked, the youth carried the armor beyond the required point. When the soldier mentioned that further service was unnecessary, the youth, who had found the soldier's tale fascinating and exciting, replied, "The last mile was for you—this mile is for me."

Could it be that today the story of the extra mile means making an investment in oneself, seeking personal growth, and becoming excited by the world around us? If employee passivity is to diminish, and involvement, commitment, and contribution are to replace it, perhaps we should more closely analyze the purpose of this extra mile story and our interpretation of it.

PREPARING TO BE MENTORED

We tend to focus so intently on role of the mentor that we forget an essential point: the reason for mentoring is to help the mentee increase his or her personal effectiveness and productivity. Indeed, very few organizations that support ongoing mentoring provide significant training for mentees in "how to make the most of being mentored."

Consider the case of Freddie Mac Corporation. In 1993, this firm conducted a series of interviews with junior-level mentees from the management information systems division who had been paired with company executives for one year in a previous program. While two-thirds of the mentees said their experience had been an unalloyed success, and they had experienced considerable growth and development, one-third experienced relationship problems that diminished their gains.

Some of these problems stemmed from mutual shortcomings: neither the mentee nor the mentor fully appreciated the subtleties inherent in the relationship. Most problems, however, came because the mentees were passive or held the mentor in such awe that they were unable to relate effectively. In many cases, even when the mentees were able to work through these problems, several months passed during which mentees were reticent or fearful of making a mistake. The company subsequently modified mentor and mentee training to overcome the "awe factor."

Unfortunately, most formal mentoring programs begin the relationship with either no training, or with a social-hour orientation session—a "get-acquainted" activity. If the gains of mentoring are to be realized, mentees need to be prepared for the experience. Moreover, this preparation needs to be well integrated with the organization's overall training plan. Basically, the need is for partnering skills, a topic we will return to in a moment.

THE POWER ISSUE

So much of the history of mentoring has been associated with the notion that mentors are older, wiser, more experienced, and more knowledgeable than their mentees, that it comes as a shock when this notion is challenged. Many people perceive the mentor-mentee relationship as a kind of parent-child bond. However, these days many mentees are better educated, more "world wise," and more technically competent than their mentors. Thus, it's unwise to view mentees on the basis of assumptions, stereotypes, or past history.

For example, executives at fairly high levels have often climbed the corporate ladder by excelling in a narrow specialty—such as engineering or accounting—and by managing people in that specialty. They may have spent their whole careers in one firm or one kind of business, and may have failed to learn about related technological developments, such as information management systems. By contrast, their mentees may be broadly educated and well trained, and may have advanced in several organizations and been assigned overseas.

Of course, such mentees still have a lot to learn from these mentors. In such situations, the mentor may begin the relationship by acquainting the mentee with the peculiarities of their specific organization's business, the evolving corporate culture, the efforts being made to capture new markets, and dozens of other points that can help the mentee operate effectively.

The Machine-Age mentoring model assumes that mentees will eventually achieve "position power"—the power that comes from holding a particular job at an exalted level. While this type of power may still be important, the development of *expert power* and *inner power* (the power that comes from mental agility, creativity, persuasiveness, energy, stamina, determination, vision, problem solving, etc.) are increasingly potent in Information-Age mentoring.

Today mentoring is increasingly seen as a *partnership*, meaning that mentees are expected to play an active role in their own development by identifying their own needs (to as great an extent as possible), making those needs specific, soliciting mentor assistance, and making effective use of that help to benefit both the organization and themselves.

THE MENTOR-MENTEE PARTNERSHIP

Organizations that define the mentoring relationship as a partnership make it clear to employees that each participant has a role, and that mutual investment is required in order to attain mutual gain. Developing formal mentoring programs that are driven by the mentee, as opposed to the mentor, and ensuring that participation is voluntary on both sides also lowers the risk of legal problems.

What benefits can the mentee expect from a *formal* mentoring partnership? Even the most sophisticated mentees can benefit from:

- An opportunity to learn from the mentor's particular experiences, personal insights, knowledge, and know-how.
- The chance to test their ideas, tactics, and strategies in a friendly forum.
- Insight into the organization's culture, political structure, and vision.
- A network of contacts that keeps them abreast of important changes.
- Insight into and reinforcement of specific behaviors that support organizational goals and actions.
- Help in defining their personal career and other developmental objectives.

- Exposure to experience in other functional areas of development.
- Access to special mentor-designed learning experiences, as well as coaching and counseling.
- Increased access to technical, administrative, and organizational leaders.

Informal mentor-mentee relationships, by contrast, are more likely to focus on specific areas of mentor expertise, specific mentee needs, or areas of common interest that bring the two individuals together. As for *situational* mentoring experiences, these are most often designed by the mentor to achieve a specific, lasting result. They are often short-term interventions that are delivered with dramatic effect and are creatively or incisively constructed.

MENTEE RESPONSIBILITIES

To hold up his or her end of the mentoring partnership, the proactive mentee will:

- Recognize that partners often make different investments in different amounts, and that mutual gain (of varying types) is the goal.
- Appreciate the mentor's help without holding him or her in awe, so no sense of inferiority or fear invades the relationship.
- Welcome the mentor's interest and concerns.
- Learn and practice self-empowering behaviors.
- Be open to feedback—accept information the mentor provides without interpreting it as evaluation.
- Set realistic expectations with the mentor.
- Be open and sincere about his or her needs and deficiencies.
- Communicate problems clearly.

- Search for ways to achieve his or her objectives.
- Initiate reasonably frequent contact with his or her mentor.
- Follow through on commitments and seek help when necessary.
- Level with his or her mentor about feelings that are important and/or strong.
- Contribute ideas about options for solving a given problem.
- Be willing to discuss failures as well as successes with his or her partner.
- Do anything possible and appropriate to build a solid relationship.
- Recognize that mutual respect, trust, and openness is the foundation for achieving mutual commitment to mutual goals.

The essence of being in a mentee role is a need and desire for help. Open, effective, two-way communication (along with a bit of humor) is the medium for finding a way to achieve one's maximum productivity, career success, and empowerment.

MENTEE EFFECTIVENESS

Traditionally, mentors have spent their time identifying needs that the mentee may not have realized were important, and guiding the mentee toward recognizing and closing those gaps. Yet in the newest forms of mentoring, mentors are increasingly focusing on offering information about options and paths, and mentees are playing a larger role in deciding upon goals and developing strategies for achieving them. For example, a mentee may derive help from his or her mentor in planning, organizing, and managing a career-development or self-development program—and he or she may also use the opportunity to learn how to receive and use others' help effectively.

Other techniques mentees today often want to learn include how to:

- Shape or describe problems for mentor consideration.
- Select role models.
- Develop a network of mentors.
- Resolve relationship problems with a mentor.
- Use problem-solving approaches.
- Benefit from all three types of mentoring relationships (formal, informal, and situational).
- Focus on the future rather than on failures and problems of the past.
- Select, interview, and attract a variety of mentors, to meet various personal needs.

In the end, well-mentored mentees who have gained significantly from the experience tend to become mentors—and highly effective ones at that.

6

Working Together

Some organizations assign mentors to mentees. Others allow interpersonal "chemistry" to bring partners together or permit potential partners to seek each other out on an electronic bulletin board. Some organizations ask that the mentor and mentee sign a formal agreement; others take a less structured approach. Some programs define how often the participants are to meet, and for how long. Other programs leave this matter open.

Each of these structural elements can affect the quality of the relationship. Let's take a closer look at some of the issues involved.

CREATING A PRODUCTIVE MATCH

The issue of "interpersonal chemistry" has long been recognized as an important factor when organizations match mentors and mentees in formal mentoring programs. Some organizations hold "mixers" for potential mentors and mentees in the hope that "natural" pairings will form. Others use personality profile indicators (the Myers-Briggs type indicator is most common) to provide prospective partners with insight into their own and their potential counterpart's personality. But certain assumptions may be built into this decision to address the issue of interpersonal chemistry that may not be helpful in more current types of mentoring efforts.

Specifically, the success of any on-the-job mentoring relationship depends on (1) what the mentor gives, (2) whether the mentee is able to use what is offered, and (3) how well the application works. How does compatibility affect these three factors? Consider this comment from a Coast Guard officer:

> I spent three years in hell working for Commander [X]. He is a first-class SOB and I do mean first class. He's a tyrant, picky as hell, and he never lets up, but he's also a teacher—a great teacher. I learned—no mastered—more from him about some very important things than I've learned in the whole rest of my career. I often think that he could have given me the same things without all of that nastiness, but that is the way he came—warts and all. Now that I survived, and there were times when I didn't think I would, I appreciate the mentoring he gave me.

This "stern taskmaster" model of mentoring is at the other end of the relationship spectrum from the amicable, compatible mentor we all might like to have. But the question remains: What drives the mentoring relationship—compatibility or gain?

Research indicates that in formal programs that focus on advancing the career of the mentee and providing him or her with special opportunities and exposure, mentees are often in awe of their mentors, and fear "doing something stupid" in front of them. Therefore, understandably, they regard "empathy" and "friendly chemistry" as the key ingredients in a successful mentoring relationship.

Yet in other cases where mentees are more self-confident and less affected by the rank and prestige of their mentor, compatibility is less important than the amount of valuable information the mentee can derive from the relationship.

Furthermore, if the organizational goal of the mentoring

program is to benefit from the strengths of a diverse workforce, build exceptionally creative teams, or change the culture of the organization, mentees might do better working with mentors who have quite different personalities or backgrounds from themselves. After all, synergy often results from a diversity of viewpoints: we tend to learn much from people who think differently from us and have different values.

BASIC CONDITIONS FOR A PARTNERSHIP

Since a mentoring relationship goes beyond obligation and contains at least some degree of voluntary activity on both sides, organizations would do well to make sure the experience is rich and rewarding for both parties. Therefore, it's a good idea for the organization to make sure that participants set some ground rules and develop some shared expectations at the outset of the relationship.

In formal mentoring programs, it is common for both parties to write down their expectations of the relationship in private, so they can freely think through their own needs and desires without being unduly influenced by their prospective partner. Even then, candor may be difficult, especially for the mentee, whose tendency to hedge in the beginning—before the relationship begins to produce trust—should not be too surprising. Consider, for example, an organization that encourages mentoring as part of a workforce-diversity program "to create a level playing field for all employees." A particular mentor and mentee may have quite different ideas of what they need to do (and can do) to ensure that the mentee can compete equitably. It is imperative that both define their expectations.

DRAWING UP THE PARTNERSHIP AGREEMENT

After sharing and resolving differences in perspective and goals, it's time for each party to develop a set of specific, initial objectives or plans for the relationship. In an employer-sponsored program, these plans are often developed in cooperation with (or reviewed by) the mentoring coordinator. This person can both assist inexperienced mentors and mentees in developing workable plans and ensure that the organization's voice is heard.

When the initial plans or objectives have been developed, the coordinator often asks questions such as:

- Do you have any questions of me?
- What type of help or support do you want from me?
- What, if anything, do you need to make the mentoring process go forward?

In this kind of formal mentoring program, it is not uncommon for the mentee to create a personal message for the mentor, asking for specific types of help, and for the mentor to create a similar message at the same time. For example, the mentee may write a statement such as:

- I have set the following personal development plans that I want to achieve in the next six months . . .
- I need to know more about . . .
- I want to strengthen the following skills . . .
- I think you need to know this about me . . . (In this case, a discussion may be preferable to a written statement.)

Alternatively, the mentee may ask a question such as:

- What would be most helpful for me to know about this organization or its culture?
- What changes or developments do you perceive in the organization's future?
- What behaviors tend to be rewarded or discouraged in this environment?

These questions, which indicate that the mentee is new to the organization, division, or location, will help the mentee get a hold on things that are important but often not discussed—possibly to the mentee's regret.

The mentor, on the other hand, may develop questions such as:

- What are the most important things you would like to get from this relationship?
- Here is a list of things I believe I am particularly good at—are any of them of particular interest to you?
- What developmental needs, knowledge, skills, insights, etc. would be of greatest value to you?
- What is your preferred method of learning: listening, graphics, hands-on, shadowing/observing, etc.?
- What can I do to increase the comfort level between us?
- What can each of us do to make sure we start off on the right track?
- Is there anything I need to know about you right now, such as your likes, dislikes, preferences, ways of doing things, etc., that would be helpful to me?
- Is there anything I can do to increase your comfort level with me?
- What else is important to you?

LOGISTICS

In addition, in a formal mentoring program, it's often helpful for mentors and mentees to draw up an agreement specifying a number of points, such as how, when, and where the partners will meet and work together. It is not unusual for organizations to set certain guidelines, such as, "Meetings during working hours will not exceed four hours a month."

Some of the common concerns that partners may have include:

- How often will we meet?
- How long will our meetings last?

- Where will we meet?
- On which weeks of the month will we meet, and on which days?
- Who will be responsible for setting up our meetings?
- What time will we meet: during lunch, before work, after work, or during work?
- How do we go about canceling a scheduled meeting if necessary?
- What is the best way we can contact each other?
- What ideas do we have for getting our activities organized?
- How do we alter this agreement if it becomes necessary?

AN AGREEMENT—NOT A CONTRACT

It's important that both parties understand that mentoring is a voluntary activity. They also need to be aware that the relationship is a no-fault one, and either partner can end it for any reason—or no reason. In this way, a mentor or a mentee can say, "I am ending our relationship," without having to explain or justify the decision, and without being subjected to the partner's recriminations. After all, if the mentor-mentee agreement were in any way enforceable, the interaction would involve obligation and cease to be mentoring, since the spirit of volunteerism would be gone.

To be sure, this type of no-fault understanding is difficult for some to accept. People often levy unwarranted expectations on others, which leads them to demand an explanation or feel hurt, outraged, or cheated when a relationship ends. The partner, in response, may resort to hedging, phony justifications, or even counter-recriminations. For this reason, an up-front understanding that no justifications will be given will help the parties adjust to any changes down the road.

Those who want to "hold someone to" the agreement are perhaps not ready for mentoring. They may be happier with a tutor, who would be more amenable to an enforceable contract.

The power of mentoring derives from its spirit of generosity, its altruism. In this way, mentoring is akin to love (which is often the prime motivator for mentoring): it can't be forced. However, it's also true that because mentoring is inherently altruistic and focuses on benefiting the mentee, very few agreements are not carried out or are modified without mutual agreement.

TOWARD A PRODUCTIVE RELATIONSHIP

In this way, for a mentor-mentee relationship to be truly productive, both parties should agree to the following:

- There must be a truly punishment-free environment (mistakes are expected as part of the growth process).
- Some expectations may go unmet.
- The goals must be mutual.
- The relationship must be based on a sense of mutual comfort and equality.
- The mentee typically takes some risks and shows initiative.
- The mentor's role is to help and support.
- People who are significantly different from one another may be matched, so as to increase the potential for learning and skills development.
- Mentoring inherently involves personal change and growth, and as such changes occur, friendship may also grow.

7

Training

Mentoring is like putting the frosting and decorations on the cake of personnel development: It should not be hurried. In addition, since the benefits of good mentoring can pay dividends for decades or a lifetime, the preparation of the ingredients (the participants) should not be compromised. Therefore, excellent mentor/mentee training is essential.

Overall, within a basic mentoring training program, seven points must be made. These are:

1. *Participants may need to "unlearn" certain information.* In virtually all organizations, some individuals hold archaic notions about mentoring, based on past experiences or learning. Often, aligning people's views about mentoring with the current needs of the organization is critical.

2. *The Information-Age model is part of today's organizational success paradigm.* To help people use Information-Age mentoring effectively, it's often helpful for trainers to discuss this art in the context of the emerging organizational success paradigm, which includes such elements as self-directedness, team play, networking for knowledge, the learning organization, new competitive strategies, and the globalization of markets.

3. Participants should draw upon their own experiences with employee development. Employees can best understand the distinction between mentoring and other forms of employee development if they are encouraged to explore the impact of their own experiences with being mentored and with mentoring others.

4. The essence of the mentoring partnership has changed. The notion that mentors are necessarily older, more knowledgeable, more senior personnel is outdated. According to the Information-Age model, the question of who is an appropriate mentor depends on who has the knowledge needed, and who needs it. While some organizational relationships today are "top down," a younger, less senior person may well mentor a senior individual who has less technical experience or know-how.

5. It is possible to switch roles. Today's mentor may well be tomorrow's mentee and vice versa. Throughout their careers, people may seek out mentors to help them learn or develop certain skills at the same time that they are mentoring others.

6. The mentoring partnership entails constraints. Mentoring today carries no stated or implied promises of career advancement, protection from adversity, or special treatment. This fact must be made explicit during training, particularly since litigation (which, so far, has been rare) may be triggered by assumptions often associated with elitism or a focus on advantaged personnel.

7. Mentoring is voluntary. If employees are assigned, obligated, or pressured to participate in a mentoring program, the relationship may lose its special quality. The voluntary nature of mentoring enables either partner to declare a no-fault divorce or to give of themselves enthusiastically and wholeheartedly, as only a free person can do.

ACHIEVING COMPETENCE AND CONFIDENCE

Virtually anyone can mentor if he or she has the will and something of value to offer a mentee. Both of these elements

are equally important. Of course, many people have the will, but have difficulty offering insights or wisdom that is more than prosaic. Effective training can overcome this problem, and can help a mentor create a life- or style-altering effect on another person that will transform both mentor and mentee.

This transformation often stems from the closeness and cooperation that develops between partners in a mentoring relationship. In time, this closeness produces an outpouring of energy and ideas, and ultimately enhances mentee performance. As proof, just consider some of the great mentoring relationships of the past: Socrates and Plato, Haydn and Beethoven, and Freud and Jung. By contrast, our own mentoring efforts may not seem so powerful, but for any given pair of individuals, the results may be no less remarkable when we account for differences in inherent talent or ability. In fact, it may be that the organization that gains a competitive edge today doesn't necessarily have the most talent (an almost unmeasurable attribute); it may simply be best able to draw out its employees' abilities.

Exhibit 7-1 presents a typical set of mentor training modules for a two- or (preferably) three-day mentor training program. While mentors have practiced their art for countless generations without any training (except emulation), today the stakes for organizations are too high simply to let employee development happen as it will. However, since mentor training is designed to prepare participants to achieve unusually valuable results in a nontraditional training environment, course graduates should be able to demonstrate (not just understand) the essence of the mentoring experience *before* they finish their training.

Training methods in the most effective programs often include:

• *Participant sharing and analysis of past experiences with mentoring.* This discussion will lead participants to recognize the imaginative component of high-performance mentoring, and to understand how these results are achieved.

Exhibit 7-1. Typical mentor training modules.

Lesson plans, audio/visual content, dynamic examples, and exercises to reinforce skills should be created for each module the trainer uses.

- What mentoring is and is not in an Information-Age context.
- Roles, relationships, and responsibilities.
- Have you been mentored? A self-awareness exercise.
- What mentors do and how they do it: skill building.
- What makes mentoring different and special.
- Designing an empowering mentor-mentee partnership.
- How to make the most of a given opportunity (situational mentoring).
- Key mentoring skills (including skills practice).
- Developing your own mentoring style.
- Understanding mentee needs.
- Reading mentee problem signals: cues and clues.
- Specific ways to help a person grow and develop.
- Positive behaviors to practice.
- De-powering behaviors to avoid.
- Developing an appropriate mentor-mentee agreement.
- Special cases and situations:

    — Cross gender
    — Cross culture
    — Hierarchical considerations

- Using the Socratic method of development.
- Enhancing one's teaching, coaching, and counseling skills.
- Listening: a tool for empowerment.
- Experiencing the joys and achievements of mentoring.

- *Dramatic true stories presented in an audio/visual format.* Stories of mentors who achieve exceptional results have a considerable impact on trainees when they have the opportunity to analyze what the mentors did and how they did it.

- *"Improvs" and other theatrical techniques.* These are used to weaken previously existing "role constraints," or inhibitions

that sometimes interfere with the easy and comfortable flow of ideas and information between mentor and mentee.

• *Demonstrations and role plays.* These are used to help participants practice listening and feedback techniques, which can contribute to mentee empowerment and aid in their problem solving. One group of participants, acting as mentees, share their own aspirations in a consultative environment with other class members acting as mentors. Then the roles are reversed.

• *Case studies.* These help participants share viewpoints and ideas on ways to help prospective mentees.

Mentee Training: How to Make the Most of Being Mentored

In the not-too-distant past, mentee training was scarce to nonexistent, apparently because mentees were believed to be passive recipients of the good things their mentors were doing for them. Even today, most organizations with some type of formal mentoring program pay little attention to mentee skills development.

Some organizations give lip service to mentee training by teaching potential mentees something about what they will be mentored in. For instance, if an organization is offering mentoring to participants in an "upward mobility" program, the employer may provide training in what that program is all about and what gains may accrue to participants. Seldom do they concentrate on the enhancement of mentee skills and knowledge—that is, on how to ensure that the mentoring relationship pays off.

Other organizations provide a day or two of training for mentees to ensure that they become active partners in the process. Exhibit 7-2 displays some typical mentee training modules.

Productive mentor and mentee training should lead to greater adaptive behavior in each partner and a more satisfying relationship in the long run.

Exhibit 7-2. Typical mentee training modules.

Lesson plans, audio/visual content, dynamic examples, and exercises to reinforce skills should be created for each module the trainer uses.

- The mentee's role and responsibilities.
- How to recognize, seize, and retain the core lesson in each mentoring transaction.
- How to distill the essence of a mentoring experience.
- Practice in listening skills as they apply to being mentored.
- How to interact most effectively with a helping agent.
- How to plan, organize, and manage a self-development program based on assistance from a mentor or mentors.
- How to select, interview, and attract a mentor.
- How to develop a tentative mentoring agreement that incorporates the elements the mentee considers important.
- How to use the "discovery method" of self-development. (The mentor creates a set of exploratory tasks for the mentee to pursue.)
- How to use multiple mentors: variations on networking with a purpose.
- Analyzing and confronting negative transactions.
- How to glean ideas and essential information from situational mentoring exercises.
- How to seek, assess, and use appropriate role models.
- Developing and maintaining an adult-to-adult relationship.
- Keeping the relationship balanced (giving back to one's mentor).

8

Issues and Opportunities

Once a society or an organization moves beyond the cultural lag that comes as a consequence of embracing new beliefs and processes, it will likely discover fresh needs and opportunities. Viewed against the humanistic objectives of mentoring, power struggles and the politics of self-interest may appear more prominent.

Other issues may arise. The competitive forces in the marketplace may highlight the costs versus the gains derived from mentoring. And as mentors refine the ways in which they help others, they may bring new interpersonal concerns to the forefront—nuances of the art of mentoring.

Most of the problems associated with mentoring fall into these seven categories:

- Refocusing attention from career advancement to personal development.
- The costs of a formal system, i.e., How much control?
- The "Fagin Factor"—negative counsel.
- Compensation and incentives.
- Outdated behaviors.

- Litigation-free mentoring.
- Sex in the workplace.

To achieve the gains that mentoring promises, we need to take a fresh look at these issues. Doing so may force us to challenge some of our assumptions about career advancement and the helping relationship itself.

REFOCUSING ATTENTION TO PERSONAL DEVELOPMENT

A few decades ago, our cultural norms operated on the assumption that "everyone" in business was interested first and foremost in getting ahead. At that time, promotions were either the sole prerogatives of management or controlled by contract or custom, as with seniority. Mentoring was a device for preparing people to move up the organizational ladder.

In today's downsized and delayered organization the view that mentoring is *only* a way of "getting ahead" may be a tad unrealistic. And yet, the "getting ahead" ethic is so pervasive that the other aspects of mentoring—creating a "well-rounded," balanced, more able person—may get lost in the shuffle. Some employees see mentoring only in terms of its relationship to such internal programs as upward mobility or cross-training (and the rewards associated with those), or as a way of gaining "credits" before a selection panel. Some individuals are shocked and disappointed to discover that their mentors are not sponsoring them for a specific job advancement.

While there is nothing necessarily wrong with wanting to climb higher, one's well-being has other dimensions—personal happiness, job satisfaction, and the joys of achievement in another field. The fact that there are games other than "King of the Hill," however, will not have much appeal for those who have never seen the other parts of the playground.

Mentoring holds a far more sophisticated promise. Until quite recently, upper management in business and government was filled with people who had devoted much of their lives to the art of advancing their careers. This ability to advance defined success. Unfortunately, all the things that mentoring is good at bringing forth—adaptability, creativity, imagination, a sense of balance and proportion, vision, insight, the utility of our feelings, intuition, caring for others, a sense of sharing and helping—were largely ignored. Yet today these are the capacities that successful, proactive leaders need in abundance.

Until a thirst for self-development comes in balance with the hunger for getting to the top, we are unlikely to nurture the organizational leaders needed for the future.

THE COSTS OF A FORMAL SYSTEM: HOW MUCH CONTROL?

A leading proponent of the measurement and control school of management has been quoted as saying, "If it can't be measured, it hasn't happened!"

Fair enough. But how do you measure internal change in a person—the blending of everything learned and every skill mastered to bring about a subtle shift in leadership style? How do you measure the consequences of listening to a senior sales representative talk about the subtlety of a customer service transaction, then internalizing that subtlety as part of your behavior when dealing with other customers?

Even if measurement in literally tens of thousands of such transactions each day were possible, would that make the measurement cost effective? Mentoring is partly an art form, dependent on the imagination of the participants. While the organization may have legitimate goals that it expects to achieve through its formal mentoring system, too great an effort to control the process can easily produce a paint-by-the-numbers piece of art.

Those who believe that most individuals are incapable of creativity, spontaneous synergism, and artful personal development will probably continue to treat mentoring as a simple input/output device.

Some companies have designed mentoring programs so that participants understand why the organization chose mentoring as a device for exceptional personal development and what the employer expects as a result. The programs convey the idea that management trusts people to get the job done. In these operations, costs were minimal and mentees arranged to get what they needed without significant burden on the system.

As more organizations seek to create a healthy and productive workplace and self-directed, empowered personnel, they adopt mentoring as support for their evolving and adaptive culture. These organizations recognize mentoring as a pervasive instrument for bonding employees in a network of flexible caring and sharing relationships. They envision evolution of the *helping organization* where information and ideas flow easily to the points of greatest utility, thereby making the organization (and its components) proactive, efficient, and productive.

This would be in stark contrast to cultures that still encourage the hoarding of knowledge, compartmentalization of activities, and bureaucratic control, i.e., where suspicion and animosity thrive.

THE FAGIN FACTOR—NEGATIVE COUNSEL

Charles Dickens, in his book *Oliver Twist*, portrays Fagin as a criminal beyond redemption. However, Fagin did take in a number of homeless boys. He fed them, provided them with a place to stay, and taught them survival skills (thievery). Clearly, Fagin was serving his own interests, but at least he was helping boys who had few other prospects until he came along.

The Fagin character may seem long ago and far away. I have, however, heard and observed business executives—people who fancied themselves to be mentors—offering advice to less sophisticated individuals on price fixing, questionable tax avoidance techniques, falsifying official records, lying to investigative agencies, bribery, and a multitude of other crimes and misdemeanors. These suggestions were handed out with confident admonitions of "No one will ever know" or "Everyone does it"—generalizations that can lead to a jail cell.

Most people understand the positive focus of mentoring. But when it comes to encouraging employees to mentor, they may come to recognize some hard truths: *Some folks make poor to awful mentors.* As one corporate vice president put it, "We have people around here I wouldn't want to mentor a warthog. Their advice is terrible. They are out of touch and out of date."

There is no easy answer to the problem of "inappropriate mentors." Some organizations screen mentors and invite those with poor mentoring skills to take on administrative roles, or to become advocates for the program. The best answer, however, seems to be better training. This includes both experiential training in which peers influence each other, as well as class exercises that help prospective mentors correct inappropriate attitudes and behaviors.

COMPENSATION AND INCENTIVES

It has been argued that you can't hire a mentor. Once a mentor invests in receiving a tangible payout, the spirit of mentoring departs. The freely given help of a mentor is compromised, and the organization (or even the mentee) has leverage to extract something.

One professional society has a very popular "Rent a Mentor" program underway which has failed to grasp the essence of the relationship.

The members, many of whom are frustrated because they do not have the background they need to practice successfully in their chosen field, recognized that a highly experienced person in their discipline could provide insightful, incisive help in specific areas. The program hopes to attract technical experts who can also focus on members' welfare and development. They could just hire a consultant and call a spade a spade, but they hope for more.

Similar problems arise when an organization *requires* someone to mentor, makes mentoring subject to evaluation or performance appraisal, or provides extra compensation to the mentor for taking on that responsibility. Some organizations that have tried this approach found that they needed burdensome and expensive measurements to "ensure" that the mentors were doing their jobs. Others found that they tended to attract mentors who were more focused on the extra income than on the help they could give—that is, the personnel who applied for the position of mentor most vigorously were the least likely to be effective mentors.

If compensation of any form accrues to the mentor, the selection should be very carefully done.

OUTDATED BEHAVIORS

Behavioral scientists, especially those specializing in communications, motivation, and human performance, have identified behaviors that can either help or hinder mentor effectiveness (see Chapter 4). Any mentoring program that ignores this research will produce mixed results, at best. And mentors who are unable to correct their tendencies to use inappropriate behaviors—especially criticizing, rushing in with advice, and "rescuing"—will experience more frustration than satisfaction.

LITIGATION-FREE MENTORING

Because some organizations are stuck on mentoring as a career advancement tool rather than as a human development tool, it is not surprising that the proteges play the Machine-Age games of comparing the power, prestige, and position of their mentors with those "assigned" to others and believe that they have come up short. This "disparate mentoring," as they see it, has led to a few lawsuits (so far) and even to some courts (where the old notions of mentoring hold sway) taking the charges seriously. (See box, page 81)

Disparate Mentoring

In 1993, the U.S. District Court for Maryland ruled that a female psychiatrist may pursue a claim of "disparate mentoring" under Title VII of the Civil Rights Act. In the psychiatrist's suit, she alleged that, compared with her male peers, she received less mentoring and feedback in a fellowship program at the National Institutes for Mental Health in Bethesda, Maryland. She also claimed that the difference in mentoring was motivated by "sexual animus."

The court rejected a recommendation to dismiss the suit and ruled that mentoring could be considered a "term, condition, and privilege of employment," similar to job assignments and training opportunities.

"Unfortunately," said Laurie Rabideau, Director of the Mentor Foundation, "the Judge was apparently reacting to the way mentoring was practiced in that organization. Some changes in philosophy, goals, practices, and training would have created a mentoring system so fair as to be virtually immune to successful legal action." At the time of writing, the case has not been resolved.

However, when the mentoring relationship is a partnership of equals, where the mentee sets the agenda and initiates the connection, where the mentee is to make things happen, where the relationship is voluntary and free on both sides, and where either party can terminate for any reason or no reason, there is virtually no basis for a lawsuit unless either party (or both) is involved in something that has nothing to do with mentoring.

SEX IN THE WORKPLACE

We can be reasonably certain that workplace romance has been around as long as there has been a workplace. Sexual issues in the workplace have become more complex, and hopefully, with sexual harassment legislation, less common and less focused on the extraction of favors in either direction.

A decade or so ago, the media gave sensational coverage to a few cases that were tied directly to mentoring as the lure or at least the incipient incident. However, all of those cases were based on relationships where career climbing, favoritism, and extraordinary treatment were part of the scenario. If the same events happened in the newer mentoring environment, they would probably be treated as grievances by co-workers or treated under EEO laws.

Nevertheless, we do need to look at this issue.

The caring, sharing and helping so essential to an effective mentoring relationship does tend to produce a closeness, affection, and even love (sex is another issue) between the partners. No one should be too surprised if this caring produces warm feelings. However, friendship, caring, and affection need not lead to more base relationships in mentoring any more than it would in other close working relationships. It should also be recognized that this sense of closeness is often what provides the enthusiasm and synergistic benefits from the mentoring relationship.

Thus, the feelings that develop can be either a boon or the cause for a serious blunder, depending on how the participants handle these feelings.

9

Current Mentoring Applications

Almost daily we encounter new applications of mentoring—suggesting that its potential is limited only by our imagination.

This chapter surveys the growing variety of applications, both inside and peripheral to the organization. These uses of mentoring are not exotic. All have solid, productive track records in more than one organization. The skill with which they are practiced determines the value they produce.

BUSINESS-TO-BUSINESS MENTORING

The Department of Defense (DOD) thinks enough of mentoring to set aside funds for some defense contractors to mentor their subcontractors and suppliers. The DOD recognizes the importance of having broad-based sources of supply. And it wants these suppliers to be stable companies that are staffed with competent personnel and competitive within their industries. Thus, the department encourages its contractors to help their vendors meet defense specifications, operate efficiently, and even enter new markets.

Nationally, mentoring is being handled by organizations such as SCORE (Senior Corps of Retired Executives), a network organization that carefully matches retired executive volunteers with novice entrepreneurs to help them with their specific needs and get them on their way to creating a successful venture.

SCORE mentoring does not necessarily stop once the business initially "takes off." Many entrepreneurs are able to create businesses, but succumb to obstacles that prevent these enterprises from becoming the viable, enduring ventures their owners are working so hard to secure. A mentor's expertise can often provide the entrepreneur with the perspective needed to overcome those obstacles.

In the area of business-to-business manufacturing, it is becoming more common for manufacturers to mentor their customers' personnel. For decades, some companies have provided training for their users to ensure effective handling, maintenance, and repair of their products. But as product complexity increases, training alone may no longer be enough. Software programs, in particular, are often underused because so much of their value comes from applying a program's more sophisticated features to new challenges in the user's work. In this instance, a mentor can help the user explore her or his special options—many of which are not identifiable until after the user has mastered the intended applications.

The box on page 85 shows business-to-business mentoring in still another context.

TRANSITION MENTORING

Some organizations, when faced with the prospects of large-scale reductions in force, use internal and external mentors to help employees face the challenge of the transition. This voluntary support—which goes beyond the employer's out-

Mentor or Mentee, or Both

Under the heading "Power Connection," Frank Swoboda and Warren Brown in a *Washington Post* article (April 3, 1994) related how CEOs of some of America's largest corporations have been beating a path to the door of Jack Welch, chief executive officer of General Electric Corporation.

Titans in their own right, the heads of such firms as General Motors, International Business Machines Corporation, and Eastman-Kodak Company have gone to the undisputed champion of corporate reorganization. In the past 13 years, since taking over GE, Welch has cut its workforce in half, positioned the company so that every line of their business is first or second in its industry, and raised its revenue from $26 billion to more than $60 billion.

Swoboda and Brown refer to the meetings as the "CEO's Club," and say that this type of contact makes a larger point about managing in the '90s. "In today's increasingly competitive climate, traditionally inbred corporations are being forced to look outside to keep up with the best business practices." Many CEO contacts are by phone, and it is not uncommon for Welch to invite them over to share ideas. Welch has constantly preached the need for executives to get outside their own organizations to see what works best and then to borrow those techniques or ideas. Welch spends much time personally visiting other companies. Consequently, Welch's attitude makes it easier for other executives to seek him out. This is Information-Age networking at its most productive.

But, of greater significance here is that these meetings and telephone calls represent a series of classic mentoring sessions, with Welch as the mentor and the other CEOs—for the moment—as mentees. Of course, no one calls it mentoring. Memories of proteges, sponsorships, and older and wiser relationships still hang heavy in the air.

placement services—not only helps the individuals who leave, but also has a notable positive effect on the survivors. They see their organization as a more caring and helpful place.

In a similar manifestation, terminated employees who subsequently find new employment form support groups for those who have been recently laid off. Those veterans of downsizing are able to share skills and knowledge that point others to new careers or reemployment.

Because it is now common for individuals to make multiple job changes within their lifetimes, mentors can also assist people in reexamining their aspirations, goals, and levels of satisfaction. This assistance can lead to a new career within the organization or with a new employer. Once frowned upon or thwarted by management, these career shifts often create an invigorated, enthusiastic employee who brings refreshing ideas, new perspectives, and even innovative approaches to the job. Mentors also help their associates approach their work with a different perspective.

MENTORING IN THE COMMUNITY

There have always been individuals, scattered through all societies, who invested personal energy in helping others achieve more than they would have without that help. When a retiree says, "I raised my children—I'm mentoring my grandchildren," he is making an important statement. He is saying that he provided his children with their physical and survival needs— but allowed the schools and other social institutions to round out their development. He now recognizes that there are aspects of character development—values, social behavior, creativity, compassion—that should not be entrusted to strangers. While some grandparents are raising grandkids, more of that generation recognize that they must also invest in their "development."

Also, more individuals are seeing a need to contribute time, effort, and even talent in helping the young people in their communities. Individuals have long seized specific opportunities to help a young person gain new vision of life's potential, and to help that person succeed despite life's obstacles. This type of helpful intervention is becoming more common and systematic.

WITHIN THE ORGANIZATION

Much of the recent growth in mentoring has come through the proliferation of mentoring activities sponsored or managed by the organization to advance the agendas of specific individuals or groups, or to meet intensified organizational needs. Examples include:

• *Entry-Level Personnel.* In the past, a few of the larger, more stable organizations welcomed the arrival of special groups of newly hired management or technical college graduates (mostly scientists or engineers) as interns entitled to a period of mentoring. In more recent times, companies are adding groups of apprentices and skilled technicians—as well as experienced personnel and even managers who are entering a new corporate culture—to the ranks of formal mentoring programs.

• *Career Enhancement Programs.* As organizations move from steeply sloped pyramids and ladder structures to the pancake model, they become more aware of the career needs of virtually all employees. The career-building programs of today, many of which warrant the help of a mentor, tend to be more systematic and modeled on a mentor/mentee partnership—such as when individual development plans (IDPs) are used to chart advancement.

• *Breaking Through the Glass Ceiling.* Today's proliferation of "women's programs" provides an excellent example of special-purpose mentoring. These programs aim at achieving a more balanced technical and managerial workforce, as the discussion in Chapter 1 shows.

- *Workforce Diversity.* Similar in focus are those programs designed to create a level playing field for members of racial and ethnic minorities. By enabling diverse groups to participate and contribute more equally to the advancement of the organization, more people benefit. Diversity programs respond to the fact that the workforce *is* becoming more varied and that mentoring is one way to ensure that we move from an exclusive hierarchy to a more open and equitable one.

- *Team Building.* As a company changes from a highly individualistic and competitive work environment to a more cooperative team culture, employees may find that they don't know how to be truly cooperative and trusting. While training in teamwork and group problem-solving processes help a great deal, many organizations are also developing mentors to help team members (and some managers) get over their competitive "hang-ups," which interfere with group synergy.

- *TQM Efforts.* Total quality management (TQM) is a sound concept and critical to America's competitiveness here and abroad. At the same time, however, the emphasis on control of people and machines, as well as the need to measure everything with statistics, can become so burdensome as to stifle originality. In some cases, the obsession with proving results (alleged gains) has raised costs and imperiled the program. As an antidote, some organizations are empowering mentors to work with individuals and teams alike to streamline their efforts, reduce costs, and rekindle enthusiasm. TQM enthusiasts, experts, and advocates are often cast in the mentoring role.

- *Conserving Organizational Memory and Know-How.* Many organizations are realizing the consequences of losing skilled and knowledgeable people through precipitous downsizing and early retirement windows. It is becoming increasingly common for these organizations to ask the departing employees to cross-train and mentor those people who remain.

- *Rebuilding Organizational Trust.* Downsizing also erodes the basis for employee trust. Some organizations find that well-trained mentors are a viable linking device in rebuilding and maintaining this important element of organizational culture. Even though the trust that develops is often interpersonal (rather than institutional, as it used to be), surviving employees tend to feel less alienated, more "in" on things, and in some ways more secure when they have a mentor to help them address their concerns and problems. The sincere helpfulness of an effective mentor can recreate an environment of trust.

• *Accelerated Transfer of Technical Skills and Knowledge.* In today's fast-paced environment—where "Speed is Life," as Tom Peters is fond of saying—people need to "fill the cracks" in their knowledge and skills as rapidly as possible. A technical mentoring network not only enhances their efforts to master their field but also strengthens their ability to adapt to rapidly evolving technology and change. Transfer of technical know-how is one of the oldest forms of mentoring and is growing more critical each day.

• *Leadership Development.* Some leaders have always used mentoring to enhance the competence and performance of those they lead. The great leaders have tended to do this with exceptional skill and grace. But we are now moving away from the notion of leader as an all-knowing commander to the recognition that, in the Information Age, organizational success is built on the cumulative effect of tens of thousands of less majestic decisions. A myriad of mentors operating throughout the organization can improve the quality and beneficial effect of those decisions. Today, effective leaders regard personal mentoring—and encouraging those who are mentored to expand the circle—as one of their greatest opportunities to invest in building a successful organization. The list of innovative uses of mentoring presented here is far from complete. As a basic component of one-on-one employee development, this variety of applications is almost certain to grow in number and quality.

About the Author

Gordon F. Shea serves as president of PRIME Systems Company, a training and human resource development firm in the Washington-Baltimore area. Prior to launching his own firm, he worked as a supervisor, manager, and executive in government and private industry for 25 years. Mr. Shea earned degrees from Syracuse University and George Washington University.

Beginning his career as a technical writer and industrial engineer, he climbed the ranks in corporations such as Honeywell and Litton Industries, eventually becoming vice president of engineering for a broad-based management consulting firm.

Mr. Shea's training and consulting clients, numbering over

500, include corporations such as IBM, Exxon, and Singer-Link; governmental agencies such as the National Aeronautics and Space Administration, the National Institutes of Health, and the United States Departments of Transportation, Defense, and Agriculture; professional associations such as the National Association of Media Executives; and major universities such as Cornell and Georgetown.

In addition to previously writing three AMA management briefings, *Building Trust in the Workplace* (1984), *Company Loyalty: Earning It, Keeping It* (1987), and *Practical Ethics* (1988), Mr. Shea is author or coauthor of twelve books on management, including a self-study/training workbook titled *Mentoring—A Practical Guide* (Crisp Publications 1992). Mr. Shea also contributed the chapter on mentoring in *AMA's Human Resources Management Development Handbook* (1994).

For additional copies of **Mentoring: Helping Employees Reach Their Full Potential**

> **CALL: 1-800-262-9699**   OR

> Write to: AMA Publication Services
> P.O. Box 319
> Saranac Lake, NY 12983

Ask for Stock #02357XMPR. $14.95 per single copy/AMA Members $13.45. Substantial discounts for bulk orders (11 or more copies).

OTHER AMA MANAGEMENT BRIEFINGS OF INTEREST

Blueprints for Service Quality: The Federal Express Approach, SECOND EDITION

Detailed, how-to information on personnel practices and quality measurement systems at Federal Express. Recently updated. Stock #02347XMPR, $12.50/$11.25 AMA Members.

Quality Alone Is Not Enough

Puts quality improvement programs into perspective and provides tools for measuring quality, linking time and quality, and achieving the shortest path to quality. Stock #02349XMPR, $10.00/$9.00 AMA Members.

Blueprints for Continuous Improvement: Lessons from the Baldrige Winners

Examines the strategies, tools, and techniques used by companies that have won the Baldrige Quality Award in recent years. Stock #02352XMPR, $10.00/$9.00 AMA Members.

The New Teamwork: Developing and Using Cross-Function Teams

Organizations need teamwork within departments as well as between departments. This briefing explains why a broader kind of teamwork is necessary and presents "tools" for building a "team-based organization." Stock #02353XMPR, $12.50/$11.25 AMA Members.

Please complete the **ORDER FORM** on the following page. For faster service, **FAX** your order to: **(518) 891-0368.**

PERIODICALS ORDER FORM

Substantial discounts for bulk orders (11 or more copies).

Please send me the following:

☐ ____ copies of **Mentoring: Helping Employees Reach Their Full Potential,** Stock #02357XMPR, $14.95/AMA Members $13.45.

☐ ____ copies of **Blueprints for Service Quality: The Federal Express Approach, SECOND EDITION,** Stock #02347XMPR, $12.50/$11.25 AMA Members.

☐ ____ copies of **Quality Alone Is Not Enough,** Stock #02349XMPR, $10.00/$9.00 AMA Members.

☐ ____ copies of **Blueprints for Continuous Improvement: Lessons from the Baldrige Winners,** Stock #02352XMPR, $10.00/$9.00 AMA Members.

☐ ____ copies of **The New Teamwork: Developing and Using Cross-Function Teams,** Stock #02353XMPR, $12.50/$11.25 AMA Members.

Name: _____

Title: _____

Organization: _____

Street Address: _____

City, State, Zip: _____

Phone: (   ) _____

Signature: _____

Please add appropriate sales tax and include $3.75 for shipping and handling.

☐ Payment enclosed.   ☐ Bill me.

AMA'S NO-RISK GUARANTEE: If for any reason you are not satisfied, we will credit the purchase price toward another product or refund your money. No hassles. No loopholes. Just excellent service. That is what AMA is all about.

> AMA Publication Services
> P.O. Box 319
> Saranac Lake, NY 12983